THE CHERRY TREE

THE CHERRY TREE

THE NEW MINACK CHRONICLE

an autobiography by

Derek Tangye

WITH LINE DRAWINGS BY
JEAN NICOL TANGYE

London
MICHAEL JOSEPH

First published in Great Britain by Michael Joseph Ltd
27 Wright's Lane, Kensington, London W8
1986

British Library Cataloguing in Publication Data

Tangye, Derek
The cherry tree: an autobiography.
1. Tangye, Derek   2. England—Biography
I. Title
942.3′7082′0924   CT788.T27

ISBN 0 7181 2741 2

To Jeannie, my love always

A day lent, a day that comes between a period of stormy weather, or of fog, or of drizzle, a day like this first day of October when I was sitting on the white seat, a few yards of grey chippings between me and the cherry tree; a day of peace and sunshine and a blue sky, a day when a break in the rhythm of one's life cannot be imagined.

I had planted the cherry tree when my mother died. I planted other trees then as well, a red flowering hawthorn, for instance, close to Monty's Leap; and its red flowers hang in clusters on prickly branches over the edge of the little stream when May comes. At the bottom of our cliff I planted a solitary palm tree. This palm tree grew in one of the meadows where we pick our earliest commercial daffodils, its fronds sprouting like those of a palm tree in a South Sea island; and it became a landmark for mackerel fishermen and crabbers as they worked offshore in their little boats.

But the palm tree died on the night of the Mousehole lifeboat disaster. It was killed by the hurricane which raged from the south on that terrible night. The fronds were scattered by the wind. Some I found high up on the cliff, and only the trunk was left standing, gaunt.

I left it forlornly standing there all through the following year and the next, as a form of memorial to those who died on that night.

Two years later, on the anniversary of the disaster, a

similar hurricane raged . . . and blew the trunk down.

The cherry tree is of the Japanese variety, a flowering cherry tree which bears no fruit. It was a sapling, small enough to hold in my hand when I planted it; and now, after the years between, it has become a splendid sight in early summer, an umbrella of branches and pink flowers. Then, when the winds come, the petals cover the grey chippings like confetti.

The chippings spread over the area where a car draws up. On one side, facing the winding lane, is the cherry tree with the cottage behind it and three small beds of flowers below it, this year containing salvia, Busy Lizzies and pansies. Opposite is the old barn used partly as the donkey stable, the stone of its walls bound together by clay, and pock-marked by holes where the clay has decayed and where sparrows have made holes in which to nest.

On the left, as you look up the little slope past the cherry tree to the cottage, is the gate which leads to the field where Fred the donkey was born; and to the daffodil fields, and the coastal path which runs through some of them; and then on down the steps to the little meadows which we created when first we came to Minack.

Alongside the end wall, to the left, is a short fence guarding the stable yard. The fence (with an entrance gate in the middle) enables the donkeys, first Penny and Fred, now Fred and Merlin, to be corralled. Merlin came to Minack a few months after Penny had died. He was a young donkey with distinguished forebears, unlike Fred whose father was unknown. Merlin was registered in the Stud Book of the Donkey Breed Society –Mingoose Merlin sired by Romany of Hunters Brook out of Jenny Jingle Bells of Oakfield. Such a high sounding background did not mean he was more handsome than Fred. Indeed he was not. Fred looks like a thoroughbred despite the fact he is not considered worthy of an entry in a Stud Book.

When they are corralled they have the stable part of the barn to go into, and this they do in extreme winter weather, or in summer when flies cause them much distress. There is

2

also the field known as the 'stable field', in which they can roam by walking through a narrow gap opposite the fence. An interesting field, incidentally. It contains a variety of daffodil called Cromwell, reputed to have been planted there at the beginning of the century. They still bloom profusely, though commercially they are of no value. The market requires up to date varieties.

Behind the cherry tree is an apple tree, behind the apple tree an *olearia solandri*, behind the *olearia solandri* a *cupressus macrocarpa*; and their branches merge into each other. They represent an example of bad gardening. I should have pruned each of them ages ago, just as I should have pruned the apple and pear trees in the small orchard.

I am, however, loth to prune. I do not like cutting branches, and in any case I have never been able to grasp the way in which one should prune. Why prune a branch which looks so healthy? What guarantee is there that, as a result, more fruit will appear next year? My instinct is to leave it to nature to make a decision. It is also my instinct not to spray fruit trees against the multitude of insects and fungi which are supposed to threaten them. I leave our fruit trees to look after themselves, no manufactured poison for them; and although sometimes there is a poor harvest, there is also sometimes a bumper one. What I have often observed is that a bumper harvest comes to spray users and non-spray users alike. Spraying has not been the influence.

The *cupressus macrocarpa*, however, concerns me. It has concerned Jeannie and me since we realised the Mediterranean heather we believed we had obtained was, in fact, a *cupressus macrocarpa*. It took us three years to discover the mistake. The heather should have developed into a large, scented bush. Our heather had grown into a tree.

Such a fine tree, with its spreading evergreen branches, would have been a cause for rejoicing had it been growing in any other situation. Unfortunately it was placed just below the bridge, a small patio we call the bridge because, when standing there, we look out on a panorama of a view, just as if we were on the bridge of a ship. We can see the expanse of Mount's Bay, the long stretch of the Lizard, Mullion, the Goonhilly Space Station, Porthleven, Culdrose Naval Air Station, Prah Sands, one of the last great bays of the world where the coastline is not littered with high-rise apartments and hotels.

We also look out on the other side of the valley, which we call 'Oliver land' after the black cat which came into our lives after first seeing it on the other side of the valley, in a corner of the field called the 'clover field', where it pounced on a potential victim, and missed. It is, for the most part, an area of bracken covered moorland, a haven in summer for nesting whitethroats from Africa, a wild area where foxes and badgers live unmolested, where pheasants linger without fear of being shot, an area where there is a multitude of insects and butterflies, an area for dreamers to wander along the narrow tracks I have made, hemmed in by undergrowth.

To the left of this moorland is the large field, the clover field, where the donkeys often graze. Once upon a time we could look upon this field from the bridge, but not any more.

We can only see a fraction of it. The *cupressus macrocarpa* blocks the rest, the massive ever growing *macrocarpa*. What are we to do? Two years ago a tree expert told us a gale would soon blow it down because it was planted on a slope. There have been many gales since then, and it is still there. Meanwhile it grows higher and higher, wider and wider; and I remain inert. I am unable to take action. I am unable to cut down such a splendid unwanted tree.

There are, however, two shrubs in the neighbourhood of the cottage which I am prepared to cut down. As yet, laziness has stopped me doing so in one case, Jeannie's veto in the other.

The escallonia which slopes up beside the path to the bridge involves my laziness. There are two varieties of escallonia on this slope, and one of them suffers severely from the dry soil of summer; and as a result it has become increasingly woody, so that the evergreen leaves which ought to be there are absent for the most part.

The second escallonia variety, on the other hand, a broader leaved variety, burgeons. We call it 'escallonia towers', because within its upper branches are the night time sleeping quarters of local dunnocks, and a blackbird or two, while at ground level it has always been a hideout for the cats of Minack; and also a restaurant where a captured rabbit is demolished. This escallonia, with its sweet-smelling, little rose-coloured flowers, gives me no problem. But I look at the woody escallonia every day, aware that I should act, yet I remain immobile.

The other shrub I was prepared to cut down, I could see while I sat on the white seat that first day of October, a day lent. It was to the right of the cherry tree as I faced it, a sprawling, untidy fuschia which, in its heyday, had bell-like white and pink flowers, but had been sterile for three years. I had urged Jeannie to let me slash it to the ground, dig up the roots, throw it away; and for three years she had refused to let me. The garden is her preserve so I had to obey, for she had put her faith in the belief that one day the fuschia would start flowering again.

There was another reason for her reluctance to let me slash at it. I have a poor record when acting on my own initiative in the garden. I am accident prone. One such accident occurred this spring, when I set out to cut down the brambles which had become intertwined with the beautiful white climbing rose which enveloped the stone wall of the so-called garage. Instead of selecting the thick, main stems of the brambles to cut with my secateurs, I made the mistake of muddling them with those of the climbing rose. Hence, Jeannie was later to tell me that I had cut the stems of the rose instead of those of the brambles. She was quite gentle about it.

I was sitting there on the white seat when Ambrose came nonchalantly down the path from the cottage and then, within a few yards of me, turned upside down, curling his paws, swaying on his back to and fro, inviting me, it would appear, to leave the white seat and tickle him. Yet I knew from experience that if I did so he would race away from me. His thoughts, as often happens to all of us, did not coincide with reality.

He had other foibles, and one of them gave me satisfaction. A reason why for so long in my life I was anti-cat, was due to my distaste for the way cat lovers fawned on cats, using idiotic noises to do so; and the way cats fawned on the cat lovers. Ambrose, however, was not such a cat. I have watched cat lover after cat lover employing every possible cat lover coaxing wile without obtaining a flicker of response from Ambrose. For Ambrose has an in-depth distrust of the human race.

I first saw him as a kitten, coming out of the undergrowth a few yards from Monty's Leap, the little stream at the entrance to Minack. I was astonished both by the sight of him, and by the fact he was the colour of autumn bracken, the colour of Monty who came with us from London, and whom I wrote about in *A Cat in the Window*. When he saw me, the kitten raced away to hide in the ditch on the other side of the lane.

Lama and Oliver, both black cats, were with us then.

After Monty died I said I would never agree to have another cat, adding, however, a proviso that I would make an exception if a black cat came to our door in a storm, and whose origins we could never discover. Even in my most fervent anti-cat days I always believed the sight of a black cat crossing my path was a good omen.

Lama fulfilled these conditions. She came to the door in a storm. We never discovered her origins; and she curled into our hearts for many happy years. Then, towards the end of her life, Oliver began to appear. He hovered around Minack, and time and time again I had to shoo him away. I had no intention of letting him upset Lama. Oliver, however, persisted . . . and then came that morning when I was standing by Monty's Leap and saw the kitten, the colour of autumn bracken. Oliver was there too. He was, as we were to realise, the kitten's father; the mother came from the farm at the top of the lane. In the weeks, months, years that followed, Oliver proceeded to bring up the kitten who, by now, had been christened Ambrose by Jeannie; and the two remained inseparable until Oliver died.

I sat there on the white seat watching Ambrose upturned on the grey chippings, the cherry tree beyond; and my mind, empty of reasoned thoughts, began to wander.

The cherry tree, then a sapling, was there when Monty was alive; and now in front of me was his double, the same miniature tiger-like magnificence, rolling on his back as Monty used to do on the same spot. A gull (we called him Hubert) would sometimes swoop on Monty at nesting time, skimming just above him, ludicrously edgy since Monty was no threat to his nest on the cliff; and Monty would respond with a soundless snarl, a lifting up of a corner of his mouth. The same kind of incident now happens to Ambrose. The same pointless swoop by a Hubert successor, the same soundless snarl in reply.

As Monty grew older, becoming more resplendent, with a thick autumn bracken-coloured coat and a majestic tail, visitors would exclaim remarks of extravagant praise: 'What a beautiful cat!' Now Ambrose receives the same

7

praise if he deigns to appear before a stranger. Thus Jeannie and I are experiencing a repeat period of our life; and it is a nostalgic repeat.

I find it difficult to understand why nostalgia, in reality a manifestation of happiness remembered, is viewed by many people as an emotion one ought to be ashamed of, an embarrassment. In contrast, stories of violence and cruelty are welcomed by such people. Recently a book had a phenomenal success, including an exhibition of its illustrations in a London art gallery, which described what the reader should do with a dead cat. One illustration in the book shows a cat's tail being used as a dart. Another is that of a dead cat being used as the pendulum of a grandfather clock. Another . . .

Understandable why Ambrose distrusts the human race.

There are the other scenes the cherry tree has witnessed. The occasion when Fred, only a few weeks old, escaped from the fence enclosing the stable yard, then raced towards the white seat where Jeannie's mother was sitting, and bashed his Bottom-like head into *The Times* she was reading. My mother-in-law was startled, and forgiving; and when, in the last few days of her life, she received a lock of Fred's chestnut brown coat, tied with a blue ribbon, it gave her much pleasure.

There was the occasion of Fred's first birthday when schoolchildren from the village of St Buryan came to celebrate. They gathered beside the cherry tree, then walked up past the cottage to the field where there was much laughter, a barrel organ being played by old Mr Mellor; and Penny, Fred's mother, giving rides as others waited impatiently for their turn; and Fred meanwhile being plied with carrots and ice-cream by his guests.

The cherry tree has also been part of a special donkey occasion, that of the ceremony of the mince pies on Christmas Eve. We have passed it many times in the darkness, the light of a torch peeling out our way to the stables where the snorts of Penny and Fred, now Fred and Merlin, have greeted the plate of mince pies that Jeannie was holding. I was not aware then of the part the cherry tree was playing in our lives. I treated it as part of the scene, as if it was a lamp post at the corner of a street. But there was to come a time, as I will tell, when it became for Jeannie and me a symbol of magic.

There have been the people who have greeted us or said goodbye to us beside the cherry tree; sometimes when it was bare of leaves, sometimes when there were pinpoint buds, sometimes cushions of pink, sometimes when petals were floating in the wind, sometimes when only the leaves were left, sometimes when the lichen-covered branches were bending in a gale.

Who do I remember? Shelagh and Jane, the teenagers who once worked for us; Geoffrey Semmens, a champion shoveller in the days we annually planted nine tons of seed potatoes; Harry Angwin who was with us for a while, an ex-Royal Marine who left to join the police force and was to become a senior detective; Mr Gilbert, the postman and village cobbler, arriving in his rickety Ford each morning, and, on Christmas Eve, always overwhelmed by the hospitality he had received on the way; gentle Leslie Payne of St Buryan Post Office who delivered our telegrams saying, before we had opened it, 'Good news today!' or 'It's bad news I'm sorry to tell you'; Harry Payne, his father, now nearly a hundred and who has outlived all his sons, who claims he owes his longevity to an unquenchable thirst for Guinness.

There is Bobby Page I remember, our first Covent Garden salesman, who owned the Kummel Club in Covent Garden during the Hitler war, that haven for battle tired airmen on leave. Tubby, ebullient Bobby would draw up his car in front of the cherry tree some time in January, just when our first daffodils down the cliff were coming into bloom, and ask the prospects of our harvest. We used to send him Cornish posies besides daffodils. Cornish posies contained all sorts of little flowers – calendulas, violets, forget-me-nots, wallflowers, anemones; and they were painstakingly bunched by Jeannie, Shelagh and Jane who took much pride in doing them. It was from Bobby that we were to learn how erratic the flower market can be. One day at twelve noon we received a telegram from him telling us to stop sending daffodils. Three hours later we had another telegram which read: 'Send all you can.'

Jeannie and I, in the beginning when we left a sophisticated city life, Jeannie as Press Officer of the Savoy Hotel Group, me in MI5, to live in this untamed corner of Cornwall, had no pre-planned idea of how we were going to survive. We were looking for peace of mind, a lifestyle far removed from the London routine of our lives, the rush of it, the surface standards, the split-second pleasures sacrificing integrity, all the razzmatazz which people indulge in so as to maintain their place in the rat race. But we had no idea how we were going to survive. We kept ourselves buoyant by constantly creating new plans or, more accurately, new hopes.

Early market potatoes were our first hope. A sequence of horrible weather in successive springs defeated that one. Daffodils were the second hope, but at first we were unlucky in that the gentleman who sold us the bulbs sold us varieties which he himself no longer wanted because they were no longer fashionable. Nonetheless, unabashed, he came to visit us one evening, and sat on the sofa in the sitting room droning on about his life, boring us to distraction. At last I drew Jeannie aside, saying in a whisper that the only way to get rid of the gentleman was to pretend we were going out to dinner, and had therefore to go and change. Jeannie proceeded to change into a flowing evening dress, and I into a dinner jacket and a black tie. We then escorted the gentleman to his car, and waved him goodbye. Thus we disposed of the gentleman who had sold us all those unfashionable bulbs.

In due course our misfortune was countered by the arrival in their cars in front of the cherry tree of silver-tongued Dutchmen from the bulb world of Holland. It was during a period when solid Cornish farmers who normally were only concerned with cattle, broccoli, spring cabbage, potatoes and turnips, had observed that their horticultural neighbours were making money out of new variety daffodils. The Dutchmen arrived on their doorsteps and charmed them into buying quantities of such bulbs. The farmers planted them, but were at a loss what to do when the bulbs bloomed into daffodils; and they treated them as roughly as if they were turnips.

We too were charmed into buying bulbs, and they proved for us to be a splendid investment. The California and the Magnificence we bought are still being harvested today. We were also to sell bulbs, our unfashionable bulbs. We put them in a polythene bag decorated by a pretty design, and our first customer was the shop at Land's End. Three days later the proprietor jumped out of his car by the cherry tree and excitedly told us he had sold out and wanted more. We were momentarily confident that we were about to make our fortune. It was not to be. Big growers took up the idea and soon swamped the market. In our zeal we had ordered twenty-five thousand polythene bags. We still have twenty-four thousand left.

I sat there looking at the cherry tree and found myself wondering how long the yellowing leaves would remain on the lichen-covered branches; and then I saw Ambrose set off down the lane towards Monty's Leap, and I felt a shudder go through me. One awful day we had discovered that the land on the other side of the valley was for sale, and that a potential purchaser had already applied for a caravan and a cesspit to be allowed in the field adjacent to Monty's Leap.

Margaret Smith, our friend who helps us during the daffodil harvest and who, with George her husband, an ex-London taxi driver, lives at the end of our lane where they have made their pottery, Tregurnow pottery, world famous . . . it was Margaret who told us.

The luck of her doing so was the same kind of luck which enables you to cross a street at the exact moment that some-one who is occupying your mind is on the other side of the street. A potential love affair perhaps. I remember all those years ago at the beginning of the Hitler war walking past the Haymarket entrance to the Piccadilly line when a girl I had reluctantly said goodbye to a few days before came up the tube station steps; and we both rejoiced. All personal relationships depend from time to time on such luck.

Thus it was luck that Jeannie had ordered a pottery jug from Margaret. Margaret brought it to her one late June afternoon; and she and Jeannie were standing together by the cherry tree when Jeannie suddenly said, looking across to the moorland on the other side of the valley: 'Isn't the bracken lovely with the sun on it? Every day of our lives I say to Derek how lucky we are to gaze on that land. In our minds we call it our own.'

'Didn't you know,' Margaret then replied, 'that it is about to be sold?'

Had it not been for the jug Jeannie had ordered, Ambrose would not have been setting off peacefully down the lane. Had it not been that Margaret brought it that late June afternoon, our life at Minack would have been shattered. For as soon as Margaret departed we set in motion frantic measures to purchase the land; and we succeeded.

So Ambrose's life at this moment was as perfect as a cat's life could be. He was doted upon. He lived in an environment where no dogs could chase him; it was very quiet, no cars were likely to threaten him; he could come and go as he pleased, night or day; he had the winter hay of the donkeys to curl on in the Orlyt greenhouse close to the cottage; the bedroom window was always open at night for him to go in and out; and there was our bed on which he could sleep, pinioning my legs or Jeannie's legs if he so wished. He had no competition. He had a happy home, and the prospect of a continuing happy routine. Many people on this very day may wake up in the morning with a similar prospect, then are suddenly faced by a challenge they never expected.

Even a cat.

TWO

A thick sea mist enveloped us that first week of October, the week that the last of our swallows left. The swallows had spurned us the previous year, irked by the presence of Merlin and Fred, who liked to stand in the entrance of the barn blocking their in-and-out flight. They began a nest, then left it half finished.

This year, in May, a pair inspected the garage and found it to their liking; and they built a nest on a short piece of wood I had nailed to a beam. The pair had two broods, and so all summer we had been able to watch them flighting around Minack like dancers in the sky.

The garage did not resemble a conventional garage. It had, for instance, no doors. The site was a ruin of an out-building when first we came to Minack, one of three situated in the neighbourhood of the cottage, which itself had a leaking roof and inside floor of earth when we first saw it. There was no lane to the cottage, no piped water, and we used to take our baths in the sea. In due course, the cottage having been made habitable, we set about building the walls of what was to become the garage. Only two walls, in fact, were necessary, the end wall and a long side wall, and we built them with stones which we bound together with clay as in olden times. No need for a third wall because of a twenty feet high bank of huge rocks; and so the roof of wood planks covered by bitumen felt was secured to this bank on the one side, the two walls on the other. Our Volvo, therefore, was sheltered, except when the easterlies blew through the space where the door should have been.

The Volvo ceased having shelter when the swallows arrived. The car roof was too near the nest to ensure safety from a marauder. I did not fear Ambrose being such a marauder because he has never shown a desire to catch birds, but there was always the danger of a night-wandering farm cat which might jump on the car, and attack. Thus the Volvo was kept in the open from May to October for the sake of this pair of swallows and their two broods, four in each brood. Yet, ironically, Ambrose was often within a few inches of them. The felt roof of the garage was a favourite of his. He enjoyed sunning himself. Only the planks between him and the nest.

Sunny times on the roof, however, were over for him that first week of October when the sea mist enveloped the land and the coast; and instead, it was the hay in the Orlyt, the pile of winter hay for the donkeys, which became his favourite place of rest. As for ourselves, with the coming of the sea mist, instead of silence around us, there was the metallic note, every twenty seconds, of the Tater-du fog signal.

People say reasonably enough that I should accept the noise because it is a potential means of saving lives. This potential existed before the arrival of the silicon chip, but it does not exist today. A fog signal blows with the wind; and fog in our area comes for the most part from the south. Hence the fog signal of Tater-du echoes across the moorlands instead of out to sea. The maintenance of the fog signal apparatus is very expensive, and the money involved would be more effectively employed in improving dangerous roads. For a shipwreck on a coast in this technical age need never be caused by fog. A modern day shipwreck is due to engine failure, cargo shifting, human error, or a death-wish which seems to have been the case of the *Union Star*, cause of the Mousehole lifeboat disaster, when she crashed against the rocks a few hundred yards from the blaring Tater-du fog signal.

My brother, my eldest brother Colin, was coming to stay with us at the weekend, and I was therefore particularly concerned by the clinging mist which made us feel we were living in a cloud. I wanted to show Minack off to him in the same way that anyone wants to show off their home to the best advantage; and yet here was this clinging mist, day after day.

Such a mist, and over the years this has maddened us, has often chosen to invade us on some occasion when we specially desired the weather to be clear.

For instance, such a mist invaded us when the American publisher of *Somewhere a Cat is Waiting*, Eleanor Friede, came to see us, several months before its publication in America. We had never met her, knew her by reputation because she had recently published *Jonathan Livingston Seagull*, at the time one of the world's best-sellers; and through correspondence felt we had developed a friendship with her. She had taken much trouble in bringing together three of my books so that they read as one story; and she had also translated my English spelling into American spelling. She was to stay for one night, spend the day with us, then return to London by the night train.

An hour before we were to meet her at Penzance station the sea mist invaded us.

'Curse it,' I said to Jeannie, 'she won't know whether she is in Cornwall or Timbuctoo.'

'Perhaps the train will be late and so, in any case, she'll be back in the dark.'

'She would see the lights of the Lizard if it was clear.'

'You're fussing,' said Jeannie, 'she'll only want to talk.'

'You're right. Forget it.'

Eleanor Friede stepped off the train; an elegant New Yorker. Tall, fair hair over shoulders, a full-length black mink coat, Italian hand-made black boots, Gucci luggage.

'It's foggy,' I said almost immediately, apologetically, 'very foggy.' One often makes unnecessary remarks when one is nervous.

And it was so foggy when we drove down the winding lane that on reaching Monty's Leap, though daylight, the cottage was barely visible. But Jeannie was correct. The hiding of the landscape, of the sea, did not matter. Talk was the required ingredient of the evening, and the easy flow of conversation was possible because Eleanor Friede became an old friend within minutes of her arrival.

It happens like that sometimes. You meet someone for an instant and it seems you have known them forever. You meet someone else, and there is no meeting of minds whatsoever. When you meet someone, therefore, with whom you can enjoy 'the exquisite pleasure of being understood without laboriously having to explain', it is an occasion to relish.

Jeannie and I understood, for instance, without her having to explain, why she was worrying about her two cats, Merryweather and Lama (Lama was named after our own Lama). She had made reliable arrangements for their welfare in her New York home, yet she was still worrying about them. Very foolish, no doubt, though a pleasant kind of foolishness.

She was sympathetic, therefore, when Jeannie and I displayed our own form of foolishness. It related to a visit to

17

America to promote *Somewhere a Cat is Waiting* when the book was published. The prospect of the excitement surrounding such promotion may sound attractive; and there was also the bonus for Jeannie in that she would be able to promote her two recent hotel novels. Our reaction, however, was immediate. We could not leave Ambrose and Oliver, we said; we could not leave the donkeys. It was true that Margaret the potter, and animal caretaker if we go away for a short time, would be willing to come morning and evening, but what about the rest of the time? A promotion trip would last two or three weeks. How could we leave Minack for that long?

In retrospect I believe that we should have gone, but that is hindsight; and hindsight can go very astray. Hindsight judges a past situation intellectually because it has no means of recalling the emotion surrounding a past situation. Historians, for instance, in passing their judgement on a past event, are always at a disadvantage. They may have the facts, but they can never be aware of the emotions which created the facts. Similarly this applies to all of us when we reflect upon our past mistakes and missed opportunities. We may now condemn ourselves, but it was the mood, the now forgotten mood, that governed us at the time.

In our case we were lulled by a way of life which suited us, lulled by the prospect of periods of contentment, though we never took such periods for granted. There were too many natural hazards waiting to threaten them. Yet contentment was there within our grasp; and presumably contentment is the ultimate condition which everyone should aim for. But it is not possible for everyone. Life is unfair. We can never all be equal. There are those who suffer chronic ill health, and those who can compete in the Olympics; there are those who are permanently unemployed for no fault of their own, and those who overnight become pop stars; those who have the knack to pass examinations and those who haven't; those who are trapped in an environment they hate and those who are in a career they enjoy. Thus the lucky ones who have a chance to feel content should treasure their luck; and not spoil it by feeling guilty.

Our roots are at Minack. Yet the prospect of earning a large sum of money, security for the future, is always there as a temptation. The temptation was there when Eleanor Friede came that foggy night, and a visit to America was discussed. It was there again, two years later; and this time we yielded.

A television company offered to buy six books of the Minack Chronicles and make them into a serial. We turned the offer down. This was interpreted by the company as a ploy to persuade them to raise the offer; and this they did. We again turned it down. Then pressure was put on us from other quarters, pointing out the spin-offs which come from television serials.

'Shut your eyes, close your ears, put up with all the fuss for a couple of years,' said one adviser, 'and rejoice the money is in the bank.'

Thus the day came when we yielded. We accepted the television offer, and my bank manager was delighted. Jeannie and I, however, were uneasy. We became more uneasy when the television company began planning production, began looking around for the sites where scenes would be shot; and when discussions began as to who would play me and who would play Jeannie. What was going to happen to our freedom?

Suddenly our dilemma was resolved. The television company had applied for a renewal of its franchise. Renewal was expected automatically. No one thought it would be refused. But it was refused . . . and our freedom was preserved.

I think back now to that other occasion when our freedom was preserved, the occasion when Eleanor Friede visited us on that foggy evening, a pleasant evening which ended in a funny manner.

After we had said goodnight and Eleanor had gone to bed, Jeannie went out to look for Ambrose. As was his custom he had boycotted us while we had a visitor in the sitting room.

She found the fog had cleared, and instead of looking for

Ambrose she rushed back into the cottage calling for Eleanor, who was now lying comfortably in bed.

'Eleanor! The fog has cleared! Come and look!'

Jeannie sounded as if she was about to display the Crown Jewels.

'You can see the lights on the Lizard!'

Eleanor, bewildered, appeared from the bedroom, mink coat over her nightdress, and followed Jeannie outside.

'There!' said Jeannie triumphantly, pointing towards the shimmering sparkles on the Lizard far across the dark mass of Mount's Bay, 'You now can see the view we have from here!'

'How beautiful,' said Eleanor, still bewildered, and wanting to please Jeannie.

The fog was dense again in the morning.

As Jeannie cooked the breakfast she said to me doubtfully, 'I was right to bring her out last night?'

The fog was equally dense on the morning of the day my brother Colin was due to arrive. When Mike, one of the three postmen who take it in turns to come on our postal round, arrived down the winding lane in his little red van, he told us about the confused cock pheasant he had met on the way.

'Must have been disorientated by the fog,' he said, 'it ran in front of me down the lane and I had to go slow not to frighten it. Twice it flew into the fog, then came down again. At last it made a terrible squawking noise and flew into a bush by the gate at the turn.'

Our gulls, however, are never disorientated by fog. Their radar lead them up from the rocks, Knocker to the apex of the roof, Philip to the moss-covered roof of the tractor shed. There is always competition between these two as to which will receive the best of the titbits.

Knocker, for instance, is first served because, being on the roof, the first titbit is thrown up there when we come out of the porch door. Knocker thereupon squeaks in delight while Philip, on the roof of the tractor shed, out of sight, lets loose a cacophony of anguished cries. Then, when we have turned the corner by the water butt and are placing the rest of the titbits on the flat rock opposite the tractor shed, it is Knocker's turn to utter anguished cries.

Fog, being in reality a sea mist, brings a pervading dampness which seeps into everybody's home. It is a condition of living which generations of locals have been brought up to accept. It is as natural to them as the sun rising and setting. On the other hand there are those who have decided to settle in the area after enjoying summer holidays who are appalled; and especially appalled if their old home was in a town where the sight of a spot of damp in the house merited a call to the local council offices.

Jeannie and I, therefore, had to learn to accept the damp, and the inconvenience it caused. For instance, the limited amount of silver we possessed soon turned dark again after cleaning; and when the sea mist was persistent the porch door jammed and needed a kick to open it. Then there was the fungi which grew at the base of the sitting room wall behind the sofa; and there was sometimes mildew affecting a dress which had not been worn for a while; and mildew also gathered on shoes in the shoe cupboard.

As for those items which were kept outside, there is always the rust problem. Any machine or gardening tool will soon succumb to rust if it is not anti-rust treated like our Volvo. Thus a fog, a sea mist, is an enemy which one must learn to accept. No use being like a couple I met who retired to this area in September, then returned to their original home in Hertfordshire in January; 'Even the sugar I bought,' said the wife ruefully, 'damped itself into a solid block unless I used it at once!'

There is an aspect of dampness, however, which no one could be expected to tolerate; and this concerns indoor slugs. The manner in which they take up residence in a cottage is a mystery but, from time to time, there is an invasion of them. For a long while we were so embarrassed by their presence that we kept the news to ourselves. Then we heard of another cottage which suffered from them, then another, then another. We finally surfaced from our em-

21

barrassment when the occupier of a National Trust cottage, maintained in the impeccable National Trust style, recounted to us her own slug experiences. Indeed it has become quite usual for a conversation to be started by the question: 'How are your slugs?'

The slugs, and they are of the pale yellow variety, come out of their hiding places at night; and they choose a time an hour or two after lights out when we are asleep. Thus, if one is to catch them, one must have an alarm clock. Otherwise one rises in the morning to find slimy tracks across the carpet, yet leading nowhere.

I hate alarm clocks waking me up from an early deep sleep but, in order to be a successful slug hunter, I had to accept the necessity. Thus the alarm clock would ring its message, Ambrose, if he was on the bed at the time, would jump off in fright while I fumbled at the clock trying to find the switch which stopped the alarm; and then I would get out of bed to fulfill my mission – that of catching the slugs.

I have had my slug successes. My torch, like a searchlight, turned on the carpet, has suddenly focused on a slimy yellow slug.

'Got one!' I cry out in triumph.

And from the bedroom comes a mumbled murmur.

'Well done!'

There was no slug problem at the time of my brother's visit. The only problem concerned Ambrose. My brother was a dog person. He and his wife Pooh were at one time successful breeders of Boxers. Pooh is one of the most famous flower arrangers of her time, and is responsible each year for the flower arrangements of many great occasions. Both are anti-cat in the same way that I was anti-cat when I shared my youth with my brother. But my brother always kept any anti-cat feeling under restraint when he visited us; and he never failed to be courteous over the years, first to Monty, then Lama, then Oliver.

He even remained courteous if one of them, in the manner that cats sometimes behave when they sense a person is anti-cat, set out to flatter him. Lama, in particular, was a cat who liked to flatter. Once when my aunt, an entrenched anti-cat person, was staying with us, Lama deposited a dead mouse at my aunt's feet as my aunt sat in a deckchair on a sunny afternoon beside the cottage. My aunt, though horror-struck, *was* flattered.

There was no possibility, however, that Ambrose would set out to flatter my brother, no possibility of a dead mouse being dropped at his feet as a friendly gesture. Ambrose was above pandering to human vanity. Indeed it was his attitude towards the human race which provided the problem. He was the King of Minack. Since Oliver died he had reigned over every corner of the land, and every comfortable chair; and also the two beds, the double one, and the single one where my brother was to sleep. He would not enjoy his royal routine being interrupted.

My brother arrived on the Saturday and the fog was as thick as ever. On Sunday it lifted for a while, and I drove him to Newlyn Harbour where he wanted to see the new lifeboat, the *Mabel Alice*, which had taken the place of the lost *Solomon Browne*. To a layman she is of strange design since she has such a high superstructure, an invitation, it would seem, for stormy seas to batter her. We walked along the quay looking at the trawlers moored there; and I pointed out the Stevenson trawler fleet, one of which back in the sixties sailed Virginia Manry out into the Western Approaches to search for her husband Robert Manry, who was sailing his *Tinkerbelle* alone to Falmouth, then the smallest boat ever to cross the Atlantic; and I told my brother of my strange friendship with the Manrys.

I never met them. My first contact with them was when they wrote to me about the books of the early Minack Chronicles. They had returned to America by then, and he had published the story of his voyage, calling his book *Tinkerbelle*. He had formerly held a humdrum job on a newspaper in Cleveland, Ohio when, like so many others, he began dreaming of changing the pattern of his life. The change materialised into this sail across the Atlantic, taking eighty days, and with no experience of ocean sailing.

They continued to write to me from time to time, and when they started out on a new adventure, that of sailing in a twenty-seven-foot boat through the waterways and lakes of the Eastern United States, they sent me a regular bulletin of their experiences. Their two young children were with them, and a dog and a cat called Fred. A bulletin arrived to say that Fred had been lost. The boat had been tied up to the quay of some place on Lake Michigan near Chicago, and Fred had jumped ashore and disappeared. It has been a recurring nightmare of mine that I have lost Monty, Lama, Oliver, or Ambrose in a city; and I will wake up calling their names. Fred, however, was found three weeks later, starving and miserable.

The last letter I received from Virginia Manry was written soon after the year long voyage was completed. A month later she was killed in a motor accident; and two years later Robert Manry also died. He had had his moment of triumph, and he had turned a dream into reality. 'For Derek and Jeannie,' he wrote in the copy of *Tinkerbelle* he sent us, 'two kindred spirits who made their own dream come true.'

On Monday morning I drove my brother to Land's End. The fog was still hovering in patches but it was clear enough for us to see the sea from the cottage as we set out. Controversy concerning Land's End has in recent years been as stormy as the winter waves which rage against its cliffs. I once met the original owner, a retired Army officer, who lived in a house a quarter of a mile from the car park, which was daily packed in the summer with hundreds of cars.

'I look out of my window at those cars,' he said lugubriously, 'and I think of all the money coming in which should be mine . . . But I don't get a penny. All the fault of a solicitor many years ago.'

I do not know what fault this may have been but, in due course, the son of the Army officer overcame the legal obstacle and regained possession of Land's End. He was to sell it for over a million pounds.

The new owners, needing to benefit from their large

investment, proceeded to brighten up Land's End, aiming to change it into a leisure centre. Many of their improvements were admirable but, unfortunately for them, they made a fundamental error. They erected a large iron gate across the road at the entrance to Land's End, where cars and visitors were stopped and an entrance fee was demanded. The Cornish among us, accustomed to watching the seas pounding over the Longships and the rocks for free, did not care for this. We therefore would drive up to this entrance gate, explain the situation to our holiday companions in the car, turn round, then drive them through Sennen village, and down the steep hill to Sennen Cove, and to the curving white beach where Atlantic rollers sweep freely and frothily to stop at your feet.

These Cornish gestures have achieved a result. There is no longer an entrance fee to Land's End. The iron gate is open.

However, when I drove my brother there an entrance fee was still required; and so I drove up to the iron gate, then turned round, and took the road to Sennen Cove. We did not stay long – a drive past the Sennen Lifeboat House, the most dangerous lifeboat launch in this country because of the vicious rocks awaiting the launch; and returned home to Minack.

We returned; and I opened a bottle of Rhine wine and we took our glasses up to the bridge, leaving Jeannie to prepare the mayonnaise for the fresh crab we were having for lunch.

My brother Colin, being the eldest, has had, over the years, the tedious side of family affairs to attend to. My brother Nigel and I have been on the periphery of such responsibilities. My brother Colin, however, was immersed in them. The details after my father had died; the caring of my mother when she became ill; the caring of my aunt who, as I write, is about to experience her 102nd birthday. My brother Colin has always had to deal with the mechanics of a family's saga of life and death; and, as a consequence, he has given a freedom to my brother Nigel and myself.

We stood on the bridge and talked cricket. We have both

always had a John Arlott interest in the game, and in the past we would have long conversations about this county player or that one, quoting his batting record, recalling a bowling performance. I reminded him of the great partnership of Compton and Edrich and of the occasion I saw them at Lords batting against the South Africans. It was the age of cricket when, on a summer's day, the only sounds were that of a bat on ball and applause for a boundary or brilliant fielding. No mindless beating of a metal drum. No bawling from the Taverners Bar. Cricket was a gentle game.

'I'll never understand,' said my brother as he finished his glass, 'why you turned down that chance to be a member of the MCC.'

My father, as was the custom in many middle class families, put my name down for membership within a few weeks of my birth. Yet when, many years later, I was informed that I had been elected a member, I refused to become one.

'I've been proved right,' I said. 'You see I sensed that for the rest of my life I would be haunted by free Test Match tickets, and I would be continually tempted to take them up. My life would have been splintered!'

The fog came down again as we were having lunch, and, by the time we had finished, was clinging around the porch where we were sitting. I mentioned a photograph album at this point which contained photographs of my brother's previous visit; and Jeannie said she knew where it was, that it was in her studio, and it would not take a minute for her to fetch it.

She was away several minutes.

'What have you been doing?' asked my brother on her return. 'Feeding the birds?'

'Always doing that!'

I sensed, however, that she was in a state of excitement; and I could not understand why. Whatever the cause she was not going to disclose it in front of my brother.

I had to wait until we were alone.

'When I left you both,' she then told me, 'I went down

the path feeling sad that the fog was thick again. Then I saw something which I could not believe was real.'

'What was it?'

'I saw a little black cat looking like the double of Lama and Oliver . . . curled up on the grass at the foot of the cherry tree.'

THREE

I reacted in the way that might be expected of me.

'I hope you chased it away,' I said.

'It ran away on its own.'

'Good.'

I sensed, however, that there could be trouble between Jeannie and me. There were danger signs. The following morning, for instance, the morning when my brother Colin was to leave for his Guildford home on the Cornish Riviera from Penzance station, there was the first danger sign. She did not wait for me to make her a cup of tea, but she was out of bed and dressed within five minutes. Then, through the bedroom window, I saw her disappear up the lane with a saucer in her hand.

'She's being unfaithful,' I murmured to Ambrose who was curled on the bed beside me.

I could, of course, understand her interest in the cat. If, when living some distance away from any habitation, one has already had two black cats coming uninvited to the door, it is natural to be intrigued by the appearance of yet a third. It was also specially intriguing that the arrivals were always black. When I was a fervent anti-cat person I always acted in friendly fashion towards a black cat, almost as if I was in awe of a black cat. I had this superstitious corner in my nature. The act of a black cat crossing my path gave me encouragement. Any other coloured cat, in those

fervent anti-cat days, seemed to me to be vermin.

There had been, besides Lama and Oliver, two other
black cats who had sought a home at Minack, but their
efforts had failed because their timing was wrong.

The first of these cats was called Felix. He had been
abandoned when the farm where he lived was sold, and the
farmhouse was left empty. True, a neighbour had agreed to
look after him, but the arrangements as far as Felix was
concerned were unsatisfactory. Hence he began looking
around for another home, and chose Minack as the most
suitable.

His method of approach was persistent, aggressive and,
for that matter, heart-rending. We first saw his face eagerly
looking through the sitting room window, and when I
opened the door he dashed past me indoors, and came face
to face with Lama. He would have pounced on Lama in the
manner of a heavyweight boxer on a flyweight if I had not
instinctively picked him up and thrown him out.

Since we knew where he came from and the circumstances
in which he was being cared for, we decided to return him

by driving him there in the car. Ten minutes away by road, five minutes across the fields, we deposited him there at mid-day. At one o'clock he was back on the window sill, his eager face pressed against the glass.

This situation was repeated several times until we decided we had to act drastically. We discovered the address of the new owner of the farm, contacted him, and explained that he had bought a black cat as well as the farm. 'Bring him along to me,' said the man immediately – and that was the last we saw of Felix.

The second black cat began roaming around Minack soon after Oliver had died, and when Ambrose was acclimatising himself to being on his own. He was a small, compact cat and, in contrast to Felix, timid. For no special reason Jeannie called him Fergus.

I became attached to the sight of him coming prancing up the lane, or passing along the stable meadow, or finding him stalking a mouse in the wood. But he was not domineering like Felix. Fergus seemed content just to stay in the neighbourhood without thrusting his personality upon us. Or perhaps he was watching us, waiting to see whether a home with us, and Ambrose, was possible.

Then came the day I found him curled up in a corner of the Orlyt greenhouse in front of the cottage; and I was so excited that I behaved very clumsily. I shut the greenhouse door, and rushed to tell Jeannie. When we returned Fergus was in such terror that he was trying to throw himself through the glass. After that incident he never appeared at Minack again.

There was, however, a happy ending. Margaret and George, the potters who live at the end of the lane, had just lost their old cat. Her basket was still in place in their kitchen when one morning, a few days after the Orlyt greenhouse incident, Fergus walked in through their front door and straight away settled himself in the basket. A wise cat.

We said goodbye to my brother at Penzance station, then drove back home, and when we reached the turn by the gate which leads to Oliver land, Jeannie asked me to stop.

'The saucer I suppose,' I said grumpily.

'Yes,' she said, getting out of the car, and fetching the saucer.

It hadn't been touched.

'There,' I said, 'you were wasting your time.'

Stray cats the world over are courted, and so I could not blame Jeannie for doing so. There are thousands of stray cats at this very moment who are wandering in the neighbourhood of potential homes, watching the occupants, studying their habits, making up their minds whether such occupants would cater for their requirements to their satisfaction. Cats appear to be loners, and many a time you will hear someone, as I used to do, complain that, unlike a dog, it is incapable of love; and that it is a selfish, demanding animal which only a fool would pander to.

There is a certain truth in this viewpoint, but I think it is unfair to compare a cat to a dog. I have been a dog person from a child, always will be, but there are circumstances which can make a cat a more suitable companion.

In my case the circumstances concern the change in my attitude towards wildlife since we first came to Minack. In the first years I behaved as I had always been ready to do since, as a teenager, my father gave me my first gun. In those youthful days nothing gave me more pleasure than early morning wanderings, a dog, an old English Sheepdog, in fact, beside me while I kept my gun at the ready to shoot any game bird or rabbit on sight. Rough shooting, as it is called, had almost a poetic quality in its pleasure for me. I was a hunter. Killing provided no sense of guilt.

Then slowly, like an ivy creeping up a building, I began at Minack to become aware of the wonder of life in the countryside, and of its struggle to survive; and when, one hard winter, I heard on the other side of the valley the frenetic gunshots of men shooting, the barks of dogs being urged on to retrieve the ducks, the plovers, the snipe which had been killed or half-killed, I knew I no longer subscribed to the attitude of my youth.

As often happens when there is such a change in the

31

attitude of a person's beliefs, there is always a chance he might go to the other extreme. I have not done that. I could never condone, for instance, a politically-motivated animal rights group; or accept that fox hunting is worse than gin trapping. I just do not intend to kill. Nor do I wish to disturb wildlife in its natural habitation. I want pheasants to roam around our land without fear, and birds to nest without disturbance, and badgers to be free of Ministry of Agriculture persecution. It means, too, that a dog is out of place at Minack. I would never be able to give it the free run, the free chase, the free barking, that I would have done if I had been at Minack in my youth.

A cat, I find therefore, is an easier companion than a dog. A cat's sense of independence also enables oneself to be independent. A cat can amuse itself on its own, and if it feels like a walk off it will go. A dog, of course, will demonstrate its love to someone much more obviously than a cat, but then a dog will wag its tail at anyone who pays it attention. A cat will not do that. A cat, on most occasions, will remain aloof; and this aloofness, curiously, often maddens those very people who profess to adore cats. Such people, with their baby-language noises as they try to coax a cat to take notice of them, are infuriated with the cat which ignores them.

We have been fortunate in that we have never had a cat which caught birds as a pastime; and yet, if I wish to be fair, I do not condemn cats for being bird catchers. I look upon their acts as another example of nature's way of maintaining the balance of nature. There is, after all, continuous warfare in the world of nature, and cats catching birds is part of it.

Nonetheless I am thankful that our cats have never shown signs of wishing to catch birds; and this thankfulness has always made me hesitate to welcome any new cat arrival at Minack. I would not be able to tolerate such a cat after the peaceful times of Monty, Lama, Oliver and Ambrose.

There was no sign of the cherry tree cat that day, and no sign of it the following day.

'It's returned to wherever it came from,' I said to Jeannie, 'and a good thing too.'

I had no wish for Ambrose's life to be disturbed.

On the Wednesday, however, I went into the hut where once we used to force, by paraffin heat, daffodil buds into full bloom, and I made a disturbing discovery. The hut, among other uses, had become a cat's kitchen. It was here that Jeannie would painstakingly, on a discarded calor gas stove, boil the coley for Ambrose. The coley came in ten-pound frozen slabs, and Jeannie, the night before, would lay the slab out to de-freeze.

On the Tuesday evening she had laid out such a slab – but when on the Wednesday I had gone into the hut I found a part of the still unfrozen slab gnawed away. The hut door was shut, but there was a small gap between door and floor level. Something had got through it. What?

I said to Jeannie that it must have been a rat, but we never had previous evidence of a rat. The very mention of such a possibility turned Jeannie, another danger sign, into making an extravagant outburst on behalf of the cherry tree cat.

'It was a starving cat that did that,' she said, with all the conviction of a besotted cat lover. 'Only a starving cat would have clawed at frozen fish!'

'How could it have got there? The door was shut.'

'But there was the gap at the bottom, you silly. The cat is a small one, almost a kitten perhaps, and it could easily have got through such a gap.'

I have never tried to pursue my own point of view when Jeannie is in a cat mood. Wise for me to keep silent.

Thursday was a beautiful sunny day, and we got up leisurely, and I said to Jeannie that we should not waste such a lovely day on work, and that we should relax. It is this pure joy of being free to choose the pattern of a day that makes one a millionaire in real terms. No question of what deal to do next, no question of how to spend money to boost one's ego, just the question of whether to take the donkeys first for a walk, or to take Ambrose.

Then, when such pleasurable duties have been decided upon, then completed, there is the question, keeping a sense of guilt always out of sight, as to what to have for lunch; and where.

On this Thursday, Jeannie, because it was like a summer day in October, decided to have our lunch, consisting of Brie from Paxton and Whitfield, on the bridge. We were sitting there, enjoying ourselves, gossiping, making remarks that strangers to us would not understand, when suddenly I saw the cherry tree cat for the first time.

Surrounding Jeannie's studio, which was several yards below where we were sitting, is a high stone wall, high enough to hide the studio from sight. It was on the top of this high wall that I first saw a little black head, then a thin little black body.

'The cat's back!' I called out loudly, loud enough to scare it and make it disappear.

There had been such excitement in the tone of my voice that Jeannie jumped to the conclusion I was pleased to have seen it.

'A little black cat at Minack again! You are pleased, aren't you?'

'No,' I replied, recovering my composure, 'it's going to be a nuisance hovering around, and anyhow where has it come from? It must have come from somewhere.'

My irritation, I have to admit, was superficial only. I was intrigued. I was not, however, going to give Jeannie any encouragement.

'I wonder where it has been since I saw it on Sunday.'

'It is possible,' I said, 'that it is one of Walter's or it belongs to Tregurnow, and it's just a wandering cat.'

Walter Grose, a Pied Piper of cats, had a collection of them at the farm at the top of the lane. Tregurnow was further away, and also had a number of cats.

'Walter,' said Jeannie, 'has never had a black cat.'

'Anyhow,' I said, and felt relieved as I spoke, 'it shows no sign of wishing to be friendly. It is only a shadow at the moment, and long may it remain so.'

Jeannie was silent. Then she said: 'I have a hunch that Cherry is not always going to be a shadow.'

'So you've christened it already.'

'Cherry is the right name for her, finding her under the cherry tree.'

'So it is a her?'

'I'm sure. Small cats are usually female.'

We were interrupted at that moment. I heard someone calling me, and when I went to investigate I found a casually dressed middle aged man standing by the barn in front of the cherry tree.

If one writes books which reflect your own life, and so in some circumstances reflect the same kind of moods of other people, you make friends with those who otherwise would always be strangers. The connection is subtle. It is not that of someone wanting to embrace the aura of a pop star, or a movie star, or even the aura of a best-selling action novelist. It is a strangely intimate connection; and it may be between yourself and someone who is very young, or someone who has had experience of life. The extremes have one thing in common. Their interest in you means they are on your own wavelength. And it means also that you learn.

I learnt, for instance, from the visitor who arrived so soon after I had first seen Cherry. I learnt how it feels if, when you are middle aged, when you have devoted yourself to one great company all your working life, when you believe you have made a success of your career, you are suddenly told you are redundant when the company is taken over by a multi-national company.

My visitor explained how he felt.

'After my company was taken over,' he explained, 'I was summoned, after a few weeks of wondering as to what was going to happen, to see the new chairman. I did not have any doubt about my own position because I knew I had a good record, but I was worried about my staff. I should tell you that I had been a director of the old company for five years, and the department I was in charge of was a large one.

'As soon as I entered the new chairman's sanctum, I sensed an antagonistic atmosphere, and the questions he asked of me made me feel that the interview was only a formality, and that he had already made up his mind to cut my staff. I therefore decided to speak up for them.

'I said that they were the most loyal staff a company could ever have . . . and at that moment the man raised the hand which had been resting on his desk and, I know this sounds ridiculous, the flash of a photograph of Hitler went across my mind.

'The man said curtly, eyes cold: "Loyalty? That's not what I want. I demand aggressive salesmanship."'

My new friend was a gentle person, easy to see that. And he added: 'Loyalty is a dirty word in this computer age. It didn't help me. A month later I was made redundant. Dumped. All my loyalty to the company worth nothing. Frankly I am shattered.'

'What are you going to do?'

'I don't know. I've two boys at public school and all that implies. My wife and I have come on a caravan holiday to sort things out, doing a lot of walking. It is wonderful how soothing the sea and the cliffs can be.'

I returned to Jeannie after he left, and told her his story, and we were both silent for a while. Life seems to be running on course, I was thinking, everything organised and in place, and then suddenly fate decides to shatter it. Live for the moment, I thought, live for the day.

There was no sign of the cat during the rest of the day, no sign of it the following morning, and Jeannie kept wondering where it could have been hiding. In the afternoon, however, she had a pleasant surprise. She had decided to take to Ambrose a saucer of milk in which she had mixed a raw egg, a favourite concoction of his; and as during the day, when he was not hunting, he was usually curled up in the hay which we kept for the donkeys in the Orlyt, she carried it down to him there. Instead of being curled in the hay, however, he was at the far bottom end of the Orlyt staring intently at something. She walked along to him and found, to her astonishment, the cherry tree cat curled up in a round ball, sound asleep, and only a few feet from him.

'Ambrose was absolutely calm,' she told me later, 'but when she woke up and saw me, she bolted. Ambrose didn't chase her. That's a good sign, isn't it?'

Jeannie knew very well that my main objection to any cat infiltration was the question of Ambrose's reaction to it. My own form of loyalty.

'And where did she go?'

'No idea. Completely disappeared.'

'I refuse to believe that Ambrose would ever enjoy the company of another cat.'

'But he didn't chase her, I tell you.'

I guessed that Jeannie had now decided to carry out a secret wooing campaign; saucers containing an assortment of delicacies would be placed at strategic points around Minack. The game would amuse her. She had done it before. I remember when Oliver was hovering in the neighbourhood she left a saucer containing sliced roast chicken half way up the lane. I happened to look down that way a little later and saw a fox at the saucer, an astonished fox.

I spent the Saturday morning of that week fiddling with my brush cutter. The brush cutter is like an outdoor vacuum cleaner, just as important, even more so because, although you can manually dust and clean a house, it is quite impossible to keep cliff meadows manually in trim. The brush cutter is an instrument you sling over your shoulders, has a six-foot-long frame with a circular blade at the end of it. At this time of year, early autumn, it is my special companion. I use it to cut away the undergrowth of our numerous small meadows in readiness for the February daffodil season. Unfortunately my brush cutter would not operate properly. I had bought an early model, and it was now tired. I would have to get a new one, I realised.

After lunch, when Jeannie told me she was going for a walk with Fred and Merlin on Oliver land, I said I would have a Churchill. This meant a rest. Churchill was always in favour of a rest after lunch.

I lay down on our bed, and ruminated. Such a rumination can cover a multitude of subjects in quick succession. A long-ago memory can merge into a present-day conflict I might be having with someone who had part control of my future. A flash, no logical reason for it, recalls a time when I stayed for a month in 956 Sacramento Street, San Francisco, then suddenly comes the recall of the occasion when, preparing the ground for early potatoes, the rotovator upset, and one of the spikes pierced my foot. I was lying on the same bed as on that first night we stayed at Minack, rain dripping through the roof and Monty, companion on the journey in the Land Rover from Mortlake, beside us. Suddenly I was aware of a whisper noise on the carpet beside me. I looked down and there was the cherry tree cat.

The sight of her had an effect on me. It suggested that she was more than just a cat wandering around in the hope of food, and that it was indeed a cat who was looking for a home. Hence, when next I saw Jeannie, my attitude was a different one. I said to her we had a moral duty to perform. Somebody, I said, must have lost the little cat and would be searching for her at this very moment. Instead of amusing ourselves by thinking she might be another Minack cat, we had to take steps to see if we could find out who might have lost her.

After her inspection of the bedroom she kept out of sight for a couple of days, and we thought she had possibly left the neighbourhood. Perhaps she had just been making use of us, a pause in a journey. But the following Monday Jeannie, still leaving saucers around, suddenly saw her at a saucer opposite the water butt at the corner of the cottage. Jeannie had placed the saucer of temptation in the miniature bed of a rockery; and there, to Jeannie's delight around eight in the morning, she saw the cherry tree cat gulping its contents.

Jeannie left her at the saucer, and came back to tell me what she had seen. Then we both went out to have a look.

There was no cat; and there appeared to be no saucer.

'Look,' said Jeannie, who had bent down, 'she's covered it up! She's covered it up with old grass, like a wild animal hiding its prey.'

'Perhaps that's the explanation,' I said. 'Perhaps she is a wild cat, just as Lama was wild when she first appeared.'

We did not see her again that day until evening time when Jeannie caught sight of her on the path, and promptly filled another saucer; and placed it in the same place as the morning saucer. The incident was repeated. The cat soon came to consume its contents, left a little, and covered it up again with old grass. She was very nervous, and when she caught sight of us, she immediately ran away. A pity, because we were harmless. It was Ambrose she had to be scared of.

The first public confrontation with Ambrose came two mornings later. There may have been a previous confrontation, perhaps a meeting during the night, but this we did not know. The public confrontation, however, was horrific.

Ambrose came serenely out of the porch after a breakfast

of coley, strolled confidently past the water butt at the corner of the cottage . . . and saw her. He arched his back, growled, spat, then, when the lady saw him and fled, he raced after her. She fled up the path to the clothes line – the clothes line with the most beautiful view in the country, looking across Mount's Bay and with sea breezes drying the clothes – she fled towards it, and seconds later there were such screams that I thought Ambrose was killing her. I followed the two of them, and found the lady high up on a privet bush, looking down upon a furious Ambrose.

The incident made me determined to get rid of her.

'Impossible for her to stay around here another day,' I said firmly to Jeannie, 'I just won't tolerate Ambrose being upset.'

'I don't want him upset either.'

'All right then, we are both agreed . . . But don't feed that cat again.'

'I will,' replied Jeannie defiantly.

'Absurd, quarrelling over an unknown cat.'

Our collision of views did not last long. We compromised. The cherry tree cat would continue to be fed.

The search for her origin would immediately begin.

FOUR

There was a useful beginning to the search. Joan Johnson, a fey, sensitive person, called on us that afternoon; Joan, a helper during the daffodil season and who has helped Jeannie in other ways, came from Islington in London where she worked as a secretary. One summer day she was spending her lunch hour sitting on a seat in Lincoln's Inn, reading *A Gull on the Roof*, and dreaming how one day she wanted to live in Cornwall. The dream came true, and she and her husband Ron now live on the edge of Lamorna valley not far from us. Needless to say she never believed, as she sat on that Lincoln's Inn seat, that one day she would be helping us to find the origin of a cat we did not want. Or I did not want.

Her visit was fortuitous because she, who had a weakness for wishing to help stray cats, had a problem with a stray cat herself.

'Tranquillity,' she mused that afternoon, 'disappears when a stray cat comes hovering around a contented household.'

Her particular contented household included three cats, two of them one-time strays; and a dog. The cat in the process of disturbing her household's contentment was a stray with one eye whom she had already decided to call Nelson.

'I don't want him,' she said, echoing my own sentiments about Cherry, 'but what else can I do but keep him if I can't find out where he came from. I've called at every house in Lamorna. No one has lost a cat.'

It was this last remark which provided such a useful beginning to our own search. She had been to the places where we would have gone. She had even contacted the lady, the renowned cat lady of Penzance, who then kept on behalf of the RSPCA a record of every cat reported missing in West Cornwall. No cat looking like Nelson had been reported lost; nor any cat looking like Cherry.

'Sometimes holidaymakers bring their cats with them, and then they get lost,' Joan said. Joan is a gentle person, slim and small, with red hair and deep blue eyes.

It was, of course, true about holidaymakers losing their cats. I knew a family who were having a caravan holiday in North Cornwall when, just at the end of their fortnight, their cat disappeared. They were frantic. They had to return to their Midland home but before doing so they had hundreds of pamphlets printed describing the cat, and arranged for them to be circulated over a large area. Periodically during the following winter, one of the family returned to their holiday centre, asking for any news. Six months later there *was* news. The cat had been found living wild.

One would have thought that anyone who had lost a cat they loved would have acted in similar fashion. They might not issue pamphlets, but at least they would tell the locals of their distress, and ask them to watch out for their lost cat.

I now had the idea of enlisting the help of the Post Office. Postmen in their daily rounds are the eyes and ears of the countryside; and so they were asked to enquire (the area they covered was the Land's End peninsula) if there were any reports of a lost black cat. Owners of caravan sites were asked, pubs, village stores, all the kind of places which a departing holidaymaker would have alerted. There were no reports of a lost black cat.

Meanwhile the need to discover her origin was becoming more urgent. Jeannie was continuing to feed her; the cat was continuing to cover up with grass anything left on the saucer . . . and Ambrose was continuing to be enraged whenever he saw her.

All of us have blind moments. All of us have moments when on remembering them later we are amazed how stupid we could have been. In this case Jeannie and I had forgotten the cat world of John and Dora Phillips, whose farm was adjacent to where Felix used to live, Felix who used to come across the fields trying to make us accept him as a Minack cat.

It was Walter Grose who reminded me. I had stopped to talk to him as he sat in his yellow van having his mid-day sandwiches, Trigger the spaniel on the seat beside him, Whisky the one-eyed black and white collie sitting on the wall beside the van; and three cats sitting on the bonnet.

'Any news of your black cat?'

Often a Cornishman will ask a question when already knowing the answer; and the listener senses that the question is about to lead to a piece of information. Do not ask me to explain the reason for such a tortuous approach.

'Not a clue where she comes from.'

Walter is one of those people who help you to keep your faith in the basic truths of life. There are no desk-based theories to interfere with his views on contemporary events. Years of facing the natural elements, elements which will continue to dominate our lives despite computer worship, make people like Walter despise the fashionable views of the moment. The true values will always prevail just as gales will prevail, and droughts, and downpours which will bring floods, and the days of April when the ground surges and the sky is filled with bird-song. Simple basic truths. No one can manipulate these.

Walter said to me: 'John Phillips has lost a cat. Seen him yet? He's lost a special cat, his favourite, looking everywhere for it.'

I hurried to Jeannie and told her; and she said she would go over and see John and Dora Phillips as soon as the bread she was baking was ready.

The farm is half a mile from the sea; there are geese in the farmyard, chickens pecking in the hedges, a cockerel or two, a hound puppy mooching around, a number of cats outside and inside the farmhouse; and always the age-old welcoming hospitality of John and Dora Phillips, and their son, Derek.

John Phillips is a connoisseur of cats. Over the years he has taken pleasure in tracking the movements of cats in the neighbourhood of his farm, cats which belonged to his farm and those belonging to other farms. It was he who told us of the little grey cat which came from a farm across the valley, which used to have kittens in an old building; then, for some reason of her own, would carry them one by one across the fields towards the meadows of our cliff. It was this little grey cat which was the mother of Lama, then of Oliver; and we used secretly to watch her with Oliver, and Jeannie would leave saucers of milk and food, in a tiny meadow below some steps of our cliff. We never touched her until the very end of her life; and then, contrary to her nervous ways, she came to us when she was dying, and we did what we could for her. We buried her at Minack.

Jeannie, bread baked, walked across the fields to see John Phillips; and when she gave him a description of the cherry tree cat he appeared delighted.

'That sounds like Bob-a-long,' he said, 'I picked him out of the litter to be my special cat. But a few days ago he disappeared.'

Jeannie explained that the cat generally appeared about five o'clock in the afternoon but she did not know where it spent the day. It was also likely to appear around eight in the morning.

'I'll be over at five today,' John said, 'and I'll bring a basket to put it in.' Then he went into another room and when he came back he said: 'Here are some eggs for you . . .'

He arrived at five o'clock in his car, and the three of us waited for the cherry tree cat to appear. No sign. We waited an hour. Still no sign.

'It'll be here in the morning, I'm sure,' said Jeannie, 'try and come about eight.'

'I'll be here.'

We watched him drive away up the lane.

'What a relief,' I said. 'By this time tomorrow the cat will have gone, and Ambrose will be able to lead his normal routine again. By the way,' I added, 'Bob-a-long is a him. So we were wrong in thinking the cherry tree cat was a her.'

Jeannie was silent.

That evening after supper I remembered I had left the vents of one of the greenhouses open. There was a wind beginning to stir around the cottage which might lead to a gale, and I knew there might be damage unless I closed them. So I took a torch and went outside.

As I passed the shelter where the tractor is kept, I happened to shine the torch towards it, and the beam lit up the head and phosphorescent eyes of the little black cat, peeping over the edge of a wooden box. It was, of course, a surprise to see it there, but it was also a special surprise because it was the same wooden box, filled with the same straw, that Oliver and Ambrose used to sleep in at the time they were trying to infiltrate the Minack environment when Lama was alive.

'Let's pray it is still there in the morning,' I said to Jeannie when I returned.

John Phillips arrived punctually at eight, holding the basket in his hand, and he looked happy and confident.

'We're going to have better luck today,' I said cheerfully. 'I know where Bob-a-long is!'

As I spoke there was a black dash in front of us; it came from the direction of the shelter and disappeared across a patch of the garden and into the meadow beyond.

'What was that?' John sounded startled.

'Your Bob-a-long,' I replied.

'Oh no it isn't.'

There was such disappointment in his voice. He had believed he was at the end of his search, and that he was about to be reunited with his Bob-a-long. He never was. Bob-a-long was never found.

John Phillips, connoisseur of cats, confirmed, however, what Jeannie had already decided upon, that the cherry tree cat was a female. 'Tell it by the size,' he said, 'and the way she moved. About six months old I should say.'

This information deflated me. The whole incident deflated me. Here I had been thinking that Ambrose was about to resume his routine and that tranquillity would return to our lives; no fear of confrontations, no worries as to where one cat was, where the other might be . . . And there was John Phillips driving back up the lane with the basket empty.

This mood of deflation was followed by one of panic. Suddenly I realised an awful possibility.

'Jeannie!' I cried out. 'Kittens! She may have kittens! That's why she's here. She's looking for a place to have her kittens!'

I was just outside the porch, Jeannie indoors, when I uttered my cry of anguish. She didn't hear me because the dishwasher was noisily doing its duty, but the sound of my cry echoed to the stable field where Fred and Merlin were grazing. Fred, who is always responsive to strange noises, reacted to mine by a vibrant up and down hee-haw . . . Fred who was born here, Fred who has grown up as part of our moods, our failures and successes.

46

'Jeannie!' I cried out again, trying to drown the dish-washer, 'I've got something vital to tell you!'

At this moment my panic was temporarily averted. The postman arrived in his little red van.

'Nothing much for you today,' he said, handing me three letters, two the conventional size, the third one a foolscap size. It was this one that I opened first. A letter was attached by a clip to a batch of handwritten foolscap pages; and when I had read the letter and made a first glance at the foolscap handwritten pages, my panic faded away. I became part of a different scene. I had in my hands the result of a long talk I had had standing by the cherry tree with the dedicated master of a north-country boys' detention centre.

It was a hot August afternoon and his wife was with him and his two young children; and while I talked with him Jeannie led his family up the lane to meet Fred and Merlin in Oliver land.

He was in his early thirties and he told me about his duties, not in the sense of a prison disciplinarian, nor in the sense of an over zealous do-gooder, but in the sense of a practical person yearning to find a solution to an agonising problem.

'These boys, ninety per cent of them, would never be in trouble if they had a home,' he said, 'but they haven't a home, most of them never had a home.'

'Is that the only reason why they are inside?'

I had only been with him a few minutes when I asked this question, and I hadn't caught his mood. I hadn't sensed his dedication.

'That they are inside,' he replied, 'belongs to the past. What hurts as I go around my duties is what happens to them in the future. As they grow older there's nothing to look forward to. What chance have they of finding a job when there are so few jobs?'

The north of England, rich during that period of history when the British Empire had influence, flourished in areas of trade which no longer exist. This is the tragedy of the north, this is the vacuum which is the cause of unemployment. Yet it seems that many of the problems, nevertheless, have been self-inflicted by the British people and their politicians.

The spiritual force, during the two world wars, which inspired men and women to die, or be crippled, lay in their belief that they were stopping the enemy strutting in their towns and cities; and that they were defending the British way of life – tolerance, respect for law, and a non-political community spirit. They were defending centuries of British culture and history. It is good for us to remember these men and women when petrol bombs are thrown in city streets; and feel sad.

> Went the day well? We died and never knew.
> But well or ill, England, we died for you.

I found those two anonymous lines written in a visitor's book at a house in the village of Coombe near Oxford. I was compiling at the time a collection of tributes, by those who personally knew them, to men and women in the Allied Forces who had been killed; and I decided to call the book *Went the Day Well*. I also quoted the two lines in the book but, because the book concerned all the Allied Forces, I changed 'England' to 'freedom', when I quoted the two lines.

There was an aftermath to this book which I never cease to regret. Sir Michael Balcon, then the powerful head of Ealing Studios, had written in the book about his godson, Penrose Tennyson; and subsequently he wrote to me saying that he would like to use the title *Went the Day Well* for a movie he had produced. I could not refuse because there is no copyright in titles. Since then, his movie with my title has been shown more than once on television. An indifferent movie, bearing no resemblance to the stories of those who died for us to live in freedom.

I come back to that hot August afternoon when I was talking to the master of the detention centre.

'How do you feel,' I said to him, 'about the basic criminality of the boys? I mean, when one thinks of a detention centre one thinks of old ladies being beaten up by young thugs, violent, senseless crimes and so on.'

It is stimulating to meet someone with a sense of vocation, someone whose satisfaction at the end of the day comes from the work he has done.

'Ten per cent may be bad,' he said, 'always be bad.' Then, after a minute's thought, he repeated what he had said in the beginning, 'But ninety per cent would never be in the detention centre if they had had a solid home background . . . and a *reason* for going straight.'

'Look,' I said, 'you use the word reason, I prefer the word motivation. My theory is that motivation is the antidote to an unhappy life. If you can wake up in the morning with the motivation to do this or that, it doesn't matter whether you are young or old, you have a purpose to excite you.'

Jeannie had just returned, having left the mother and the children talking to the donkeys. On seeing us she sensed we wanted to be on our own, and she walked past up to the cottage.

'You don't suppose,' I said, 'that promoting self-employment might be an idea ? I mean self-employed tradesmen, plumbers, carpenters, odd job men, there's always such a demand for these. Obviously everyone couldn't make the grade, but at least it would give a lot of them a motivation.'

An amateur theorising.

'And here is another idea,' I said. 'All these boys must have dormant secret hopes and ambitions, so I wonder whether it would be possible for each of them to write an essay describing these secret hopes and ambitions. It might be very revealing. And it might help them to think constructively about the future.'

It is so easy for an outsider to make suggestions about a realm of activity about which he has no professional knowledge, no awareness of the gritty detail which so often stifles a new idea. But in this case I had a reaction, and it came within the foolscap envelope which the postman in his little red van had brought; and the contents deeply moved me.

They were samples of the essays I had suggested. The lack of a family base was the recurrent theme. Easy to be cynical, easy to say that each essay was geared to what the writer believed would be acceptable. Yet, as in other spheres of life when sincerity can be reasonably questioned, one's instinct has to be the judge. The essays had the common denominator of the desire for home security; and as far as the future was concerned it again revolved around a family base. Like: 'I want to marry and have a boy and a girl and I'll see that they go straight.'

I returned the essays to the envelope. The dishwasher was temporarily silent. Jeannie was able to listen. I was in a panic again.

'Jeannie, the cat is here looking around for a place to have its kittens!'

'Nonsense.'

'Why nonsense?'

'It's such a skinny thing.'

'But John Phillips confirmed it's a female, and it's been wandering around with all these farm tom cats about. If she's not having kittens now she soon will.'

My mind went back to the night when Lama first slept on our bed. She was curled up close to Jeannie, safe at last, when in the early hours I was suddenly awakened by a thump at the bottom of the bed accompanied by an unpleasant aroma. A shaft of the moon was shining into the room, and I saw what had happened. A tom cat had jumped through the open window.

'Well,' Jeannie now said, 'she'll have to be spayed.'

'How can that happen when we can't even touch her?'

As I spoke, a horrible truth dawned upon me. We were talking about spaying, and that meant we were subconsciously thinking the cat might stay permanently.

'Oh no,' I said, 'spaying isn't the answer. We just must go on searching until we find where it came from.'

'Where *she* came from,' said Jeannie.

50

'All right, she.'

There were, however, more serious tasks to perform at this time of year than fussing about cats. It was the time of year when I needed to cut down the undergrowth of the daffodil meadows in preparation for the daffodil harvest in the spring. I am inclined to put off this task for day after day, behaving like a high diver who cannot bring himself to plunge to the water beneath him.

This ailment of putting off tasks that have to be done is, I have been told, most prevalent among people who are untidy. In the case of Jeannie and me, we both have spurts of being tidy but for the most part, regrettably, we are both untidy. Obviously when we know that someone is coming to visit us there is a major spurt of tidiness; newspapers and magazines are gathered up and plonked with a pile of others on a bench in the flower house, all waiting to be burnt once we have made up our minds to have a burn; and there is my Regency kidney-shaped desk in the corner of the sitting room which is permanently littered with my personal debris – all such debris is dumped in a box and put out of sight in the shoe cupboard during one of our spurts of tidiness.

Thus we have the appearance, when pushed, of being tidy people, a temporary impression though this may be. What amazes me, however, is how some people manage to be permanently tidy. Take them by surprise at any time of the day and you find their rooms as neat as if one of the Royals was expected. Nothing out of place, undented cushions, no spreadeagled newspapers, windows transparently clean, kitchen looking as if nothing had ever been cooked there, carpet as new; and if there is a porch, boots and mackintoshes are out of sight. I envy the gift of method such people possess. They are the doers, the organisers; and when something has to be done, there is no delay in the doing. They do not prevaricate like Jeannie and me. The evening cooking utensils are forthwith cleaned as soon as the meal is finished. The personal debris on a desk is regularly removed so that there are empty spaces on the desk concerned. Where is such debris taken? It is a mystery to me – just as it is a mystery to me how anyone is able to keep a home tidy.

A decisive mind is probably the clue. I am a Pisces person and so, as far as decisiveness is concerned, I am doomed. The Pisces brother and sisterhood are notoriously indecisive. Jeannie is an Aries, bolder, more clear-sighted than a Pisces, yet close enough to a Pisces to catch some of its moods. I will say to her, for instance, how personally satisfied she must be that her drawings and paintings are in such demand, then adding a question – asking her what drawings and paintings she has still available. I then find she has none, or just one or two, and there follows the remark: 'I'll do a drawing tomorrow.' And then, of course, tomorrow comes, and she is interrupted; and so it is tomorrow's tomorrow when the drawing will be done.

We share, therefore, this weakness for procrastination, Jeannie in her work, me in mine. There always seems this blockage between thought and action; and it is exacerbated by the fact that we do not have office hours. We are not cocooned within a form of discipline.

A friend, however, has recently helped us towards solving our weakness. Her christian name is Arunda, and she is the wife of a distinguished Scotsman. Their home is in Aberdeen and they spend an annual holiday in Mousehole five miles away; and as they are very close friends we will often see them during their stay. One day during their holiday this year they were to tell Jeannie that instead of her providing lunch they would bring lunch with them. It was a great occasion. They arrived wearing traditional chef's hats, and holding a large plate of crawfish and salad. 'We are Jones the caterers,' they announced mock pompously when they saw Jeannie, 'and before serving may we inspect the facilities?'

Jones was Arunda's maiden name. She was once a schoolteacher in Wales. Ken, her husband, unknown to us at the time, once had a vital influence on our lives. Jeannie and I were broke at the time when a letter arrived to tell Jeannie that a Scottish newspaper had bought the serial rights to her book *Meet Me at the Savoy*. Ken was the editor who had bought it. Years later we met him, and we were able to tell him that as a result of his purchase we were able, at that period, to survive financially.

Arunda's influence in our lives was also useful. We were telling her about our inclination to prevaricate, always postponing the turning of our thoughts into action, when she said: 'Remember action is never as bad as the thought makes it out to be. Go out and do it.'

This is true. Thinking about something too much in advance creates imaginary difficulties. Go and do it, and one wonders what all the previous fuss was about. Hence I now use a phrase when the Pisces part of me is messing about in indecision. I say, we each say: 'Let's do an Arunda!'

We now had to do an Arunda about the cherry tree cat. But what more could we do except wait for it to disappear?

'Don't feed it,' we were sensibly advised, 'it would then soon leave you.'

This may have indeed been sensible advice, but I could not expect Jeannie to behave sensibly. She was enthralled by the little cat's presence, and now that John Phillips had confirmed that she was female, Jeannie had reverted to calling her by the name that was first given her. It was as Cherry that the cat was now referred to. True, Jeannie was, of course, as loyal and loving towards Ambrose as ever, but her attitude was like that of a wife, happy with her husband, yet intrigued by the attention of a lover.

Those who happened to visit us were also intrigued. A young Canadian girl greeted us when she reached the cottage by saying she had just seen a black cat near Monty's Leap. 'I didn't know you had a third black cat,' she added. Then there was Bertha, a widow of great charm who lives in Stoke on Trent, who also saw her. Bertha is a 'knitaholic', if there is such a word. It means that she is always knitting, and one result is that twice a year she sends us chunky sweaters, ideal when a cold wind blows. 'Which Bertha are you going to wear today?' we will ask each other.

Everyone offered theories as to where Cherry might have come from. The possibility that she had been left behind by a holidaymaker was, of course, suggested. Another was that she had gone to sleep in a strange car or van, and had then been driven many miles away from her home before escaping. Another theory was that she had been dumped by someone who no longer wanted her; and that the person, knowing we were cat people, had dumped her in our lane in the hope she would find her way to the cottage. But would anyone dump a starving cat? Would it not be more likely for the person to have come to the cottage door with a piteous story to tell? I am thankful it didn't happen that way. It would have been blackmail. I would have said no, Jeannie would have said yes. There would have been confusion in the household. As it was I still was able to hope that the cat would be claimed, or depart from the area on its own accord. Then we would be able to relax. Tranquillity would return.

The cat had now been around Minack for over three weeks; and one day, after looking through a past diary, I said to Jeannie that I had found a strange coincidence. Cherry had first appeared on the same day of the month as when I first saw Ambrose. She replied that she too had been looking at her diary, one of two years before, and there was, she said, a curious entry about Beverley Nichols.

Beverley Nichols had a profound influence on the cat scene. His writings promoted them from being vermin in many people's opinion, including my own, into being a symbol of subtlety. He invented the F and the non-F person. The latter is brashly outward, a materialist with power ambitions, or an unimaginative person who expects a predictable response from any animal or any person. The F people are vulnerable people. They enjoy gentle experiences, and they have time to observe, and they are probably emotional.

I burst into laughter, however, when Jeannie quoted the reference to Beverley Nichols in her diary. He had often visited us (his brother Paul had been vicar first of nearby

54

Sancreed, then of Sennen), and he had become a dear friend. He had helped me in a very special way when I first began writing the Minack Chronicles, though I did not know him personally at that time; and he had been a hero to Jeannie since she read *Down the Garden Path*. She also remembers the huge response she had felt for his book *Cry Havoc!* which she read at her home in St Albans during a school holiday. This indictment of war infuriated her father, otherwise a most generous-minded man. He wanted to throw the book into the fire.

'This is what I wrote in my diary,' said Jeannie, then quoting from it she said: 'After lunch today Beverley said to me that after he died he would return to this earth as a cat.'

'Oh, my God,' I said, and I suppose my laughter may have sounded hollow, 'this is too much. I was very fond of Beverley but I don't really want him around the place as a cat!'

'Well,' said Jeannie, at her most whimsical, 'Beverley died three weeks ago. Perhaps he saw Cherry wandering around lost and gave her a map, and said go there to Minack, and you'll find a home.'

'But she hasn't got a home here,' I said firmly.

'She's been here nearly a month.'

Nearly a month, and we had never been near enough to touch her, always darting away if we got close. Sometimes

we would not see her for twenty-four hours. Sometimes we would be alerted by the hyena-like noise caused by a confrontation; and then a few minutes later Ambrose would appear; and I would murmur: 'There's never going to be peace while she is here.'

Meanwhile we had noticed that there had been no tom cats around, yet there were plenty available at the farms. It seemed strange that she had not been courted. We were soon to find out the reason why.

FIVE

The day we discovered that Cherry had been spayed began for me with a donkey walk. I went on my own because Jeannie had decided to force herself to perform an unpopular domestic task. It concerned my socks. She had piled a batch of them in the washing machine the previous day, and hung them up to dry on the washing line with the magnificent view of Mount's Bay. That morning she was going to take them off the line, match them up, and put them away in a drawer.

It was the matching up, however, which was the unpopular task. My socks have a habit of changing colour. They are good quality socks, and although when I buy them they may be brown, grey or dark blue, the change in their colour will soon be manifest. The change in colour might be tolerated if each of the pair concerned changed colour. But this is not so. One of the pair will change colour, not the other one. Hence after a while, after a few washings, there is an assortment of sock colourings up on the line; and then Jeannie sets out to match them up. She detests the task, the more so because the socks often baffle her. She will end up with a handful of socks which seem to have no mates.

Of course as they are my socks I ought to help her. Instead I aim to disappear on the matching occasions, just as on this occasion when I decided to go a walk with Fred and Merlin.

'How long will you be gone?' asked Jeannie.

'I'll take them to Oliver land and we'll wander about,' I said. Then I added: 'I'll take the metal detector with me.'

The metal detector was a new toy. I had had it a week, and it had already provided me with a minor triumph. I found a silver knife which we had lost years before. I found it buried in a patch of ground opposite the stables. I was hovering the disc of the metal detector an inch above the patch when it suddenly emitted a banshee cry; and after a minute of digging in the soil with a trowel, I discovered the knife. Soon after I had another minor triumph. My metal detector discovered a purse with several copper coins of 1945 vintage.

'I'll join you as soon as I've finished,' said Jeannie.

'Perhaps I ought to stay and help you,' I said doubtfully, conscience pricking.

'No, you go off. I've got something else to do in any case.'

I set off, first lassoing Merlin with his halter but letting Fred, as senior donkey, walk away on his own. It was a walk that had its interruptions. The first interruption was caused by a tendril of the rose that climbed up the end wall of the stables. This tendril and its companions always tempted him as he passed; and each time there would be a shout, either from Jeannie or myself: 'Stop it, Fred!' And we would give him a push.

His next point of interest was the escallonia on the other side of the lane to the stables. This is a most useful escallonia because it has become the guardian of the top end of the Orlyt greenhouse. It is a huge bush now, but when it was growing, when it was still small, this top end of the greenhouse was at the mercy of the easterly gales; and there was one easterly gale so fierce, so persistent, that the top end was turned into a shambles. Today the escallonia takes the lashing of the gales. The top end is protected.

This escallonia has also experienced a moment of fame. It has appeared in the *Entomologist's Record*; and the reason is that one September afternoon I was startled to see high up on one of its dark green leaves a patch of colour the size of a wren. It was a Monarch butterfly, and it ought to have been in one of the southern states of America instead of at Minack. Hence the entry in the *Entomologist's Record*.

Fred found the leaves very tasty. He would make a lunge at a branch, sometimes break it off, then hasten away with it sticking out of his mouth; and I would rush after him and pull it away. This did not please him, and sometimes I would have to tug and tug before he surrendered it.

He had other points of interest on his walk up the lane to Oliver land, eatable interests. There were, for instance, the leaves of the coltsfoot, plate-shaped leaves which, at the time of this particular walk, were beginning to green; there were purple flowers to come which would perfume the lane around Monty's Leap by Christmas. Fred liked to devour them in quantity, and we would stop him; and then further on he enjoyed a bite at the hawthorn on the side of the lane, and we would wait as he enjoyed himself; then, because we had work to do and could not waste any more time, we would put an arm round him, saying: 'Come on, Fred, you've had enough.'

Thus it was that late October morning when I was

taking the two of them to Oliver land that the same routine took place as I have described. Fred looking out for any delicacy available while Merlin, looking out for them also but controlled by the halter, dutifully followed. Merlin was conscious of his junior status. He did not try to compete with Fred.

We reached the gate into Oliver land, and after I had tied it behind us I took off Merlin's halter; and in the delight of his freedom he rushed to a bare patch of ground, a patch which he used as a dust bath; and he sank first to his knees, then slowly collapsed until he was lying on his back, legs in the air, waving to and fro until with a lurch he turned over from one side to the other; and there was a pause as he lay there, then gathering himself he would stand up. The dust bath had been enjoyed.

Fred too had a dust bath, and when that was over I went up the side of the field, the clover field as it is called, the ancient hedge on my left pockmarked with rabbit holes, until I reached the top of the slope where I turned right along blackthorn alley. I looked back and saw that Fred and Merlin were not interested in me. They had begun to graze close to the site of their dust bath, and when I called them they did not even trouble to lift their heads. Their attitude irked me.

'Fred! Merlin!' I called out, the metal detector in my hand, 'This walk is for you.'

They obliged in due course. They came slowly towards me, and when I was half way down blackthorn alley, and was close to the gorse-covered land where badgers make their tracks, have done so for centuries, they gathered pace. First Fred nudged me, before pushing me aside. Then Merlin. They raced ahead towards the Ambrose Rock, leaving me on my own to contemplate.

I did not, however, do so. Instead I switched on the metal detector, adjusted the needle indicator, and began to sweep the path as I walked slowly along it. As I did so I was reminded of my youth when I used to relish spending hours on a river-bank fly fishing for trout; each time I cast my

60

line, there was a moment of suspense . . . Would a trout bite ? The fly would float downstream with the current, me watching hopefully, and sometimes I would spend the whole day watching hopefully until suspense lost its edge; and then I would pack up and despondently go away.

The metal detector, I was to learn, demanded more of me than just to watch hopefully.

It required the physical effort of digging. I might sweep an area of ground with no response from the electronic mechanism for many minutes, then suddenly there would be an electronic howl and, in those early days, I would anticipate the discovery of treasure trove; and I would fall to my knees, trowel in hand, and dig. Unfortunately my metal detector was generous in its howls. It would howl for a nail, a piece of wire, a bottle top, or a strip of silver paper. Hence, after a period of such disappointments, suspense lost its edge just as when trout failed to take the fly I floated above them. Yet, as in trout days, optimism persisted; and optimism from time to time was justified.

On this occasion there were no false alarms, no un-necessary diggings, for my metal detector remained silent; and so it was not long before I turned the switch off, saying to myself that as I was on my own I could indulge in doing nothing, and wait for Jeannie to join me before I put the metal detector to work again.

I had now reached the corner of the path which turns left towards the Ambrose Rock, and there ahead of me were the donkeys, Fred on one side enjoying a bramble as if it were a strand of spaghetti, Merlin on the other, nose deep in a late-flowering pink campion. They had lost a friend this year, Duncan, a coffee brown donkey like Fred. He was boss, in the sense that he always led the way, of a herd of cows belonging to a farm which had a low boundary wall with Oliver land. Fred and Merlin used to have speech with him across this stone wall. They would look at each other quietly, nostril width apart; and when Jeannie and I watched through binoculars from afar, we would invent conversations between them. Perhaps they were exchanging stories of their escapades. Duncan, for instance, could tell them how sometimes he unlatched a field gate, then led his herd down to Lamorna village; and how, on the last occasion he did this, he and his ladies arrived in the dark at The Wink just before closing time. Duncan had died during the summer.

I stopped on the path and watched Fred enjoying his bramble, Merlin his pink campion; and then suddenly, although the scene was idyllic, felt a twinge of apprehension. I could not place the reason why. It may partly have been because I was remembering Duncan and the suddenness of his death; and partly due to a story I was told by a girl visitor as I stood with her by the cherry tree a few days before.

She told how for the past five years she had cared for a donkey which was owned by a rich, eccentric old lady. The old lady, incapable of looking after the donkey herself, engaged the girl at a modest payment to feed the donkey twice a day and to superintend its general welfare. The girl loved the donkey and grew to feel, quite understandably, that the donkey and herself shared a special understanding. The donkey lived in a two-acre field a mile from her home; and she went there to see him whatever the weather. Often she would visit the old lady and give her a report. The old lady, though remote, seemed to be very fond of the donkey, and grateful to the girl for the care she displayed.

The lady became seriously ill, and the news leaked out that in her will there was a clause which stated that when she died the donkey was to be destroyed. The girl was horrified, and went on looking after the donkey knowing it was doomed. The old lady died; and then it was learnt that she had left tens of thousands of pounds to animal charities, even to a donkey charity . . . But the stipulation remained that the donkey should be destroyed. The letter of the will had to be fulfilled. And so the donkey died.

The twinge of apprehension could also have been related to discussions between Jeannie and me as to what would happen to Fred and Merlin if we both were run over by a bus. What would happen to Ambrose, too. Similar discussions also sometimes revolved around what would happen to Oliver land. Oliver land, as far as we were concerned, was sacrosanct. We wanted to ensure that it remained as it is today forever and forever, a haven for badgers and foxes, for whitethroats who travel in the spring from Africa to nest in the bramble and bracken covered ancient hedges. Oliver land is a place for snipe and woodcock to hide in the winter, for pheasants to be free from a gun, for bluebells to scent the air in profusion, wild violets to cover the banks and the white stitchwort to herald the early summer. A place for the sensitive to wander in. A place barred to the aggressive ones, those who are always harping on their imaginary rights rather than relaxing their minds in the untamed beauty around them. The sensitive are always welcome to Oliver land, the aggressive never.

Since we had this future of Oliver land in mind, we approached the National Trust. We were being tentative. We wanted to find out what they could suggest to preserve land like Oliver land from exploiters. True, we were not possessors of a stately home but we did have these twenty Cornish acres stretching down to the sea's edge; and it was an area which people from all over the world were ready to visit, despite its remoteness. People who often became our friends from then on. They had read the story of our time here.

Unfortunately the representative of the National Trust who came to see us had no knowledge of our story; and this made it difficult to explain why we so anxiously wanted to preserve the land for posterity. He was youngish, in a tweed suit and wearing a tweed cap, the country version of a city gentleman; and after we had been talking for several minutes inside the cottage, I suggested we should pay a visit to Oliver land so that he could inspect it.

On arriving at the gate into the clover field, I explained how we had obtained the land just as it was about to be sold to a man who planned to site a caravan there; and I explained why it was called Oliver land. I also told him that the coastal path went through the property, giving pleasure to many, though it was separated from Oliver land itself by thick undergrowth.

As I spoke I began thinking of the great estates managed by the National Trust, yet here was I talking about our twenty acres of virtual scrubland as if they were of equal importance. I therefore could understand our visitor's unresponsive reaction. Yet I felt irked by his lack of enthusiasm, his lack of knowledge of the years of struggle which had brought us to this moment; and although I had intended to walk to the Ambrose Rock, then beyond, and round by the path I have cut with the Condor, I realised we were wasting his time and ours. So, after we had walked down blackthorn alley, I stopped and said so; and he quickly agreed. Thus ended our National Trust venture.

There are, of course, other trusts which operate to save the countryside. Some of them seem to overlap each other, and all of them are competing for the limited funds available. There is in Cornwall, for instance, the Cornwall Trust for Nature Conservation which is soon to be in friendly rivalry with the Cornwall Heritage Trust, a new organisation.

I am a member of the former, and I have much admiration for the way the Trust has built up its organisation over the years. The object of the Trust is to ensure that all forms of wildlife – plants, insects, animals – are preserved for future generations. This involves the employment of fully-trained officers, including a full-time Conservation Officer, a Development Officer, a part-time Administrative Officer, and a back-up of forty employees who come under the Manpower Services Commission scheme. What do they do?

My knowledge of what they do comes in a newsletter; and among the items which are mentioned in the current issue is an admirable summary of the criticisms so rightly being made of the Zuckerman policy of eradicating badgers whenever a unit in a herd of cattle has contracted tuberculosis. There is also an appeal for volunteers to help produce an ecology account of Cornish hedges, a report on the activities of the junior members of the Trust, news from all the branches in Cornwall; and, most important of all, the announcement of two new reserves, one of 135 acres, and another of 160 acres, both near Bodmin. These reserves and others come under the enlightened management of the Trust, and are open only to its members and for educational purposes. Anyone can become a member for £7 a year, anyone who likes to know that they are helping to preserve the ancient areas of Cornwall.

Jeannie had now joined me; and so I suggested we went to the area which we call the 'Brontë wood' (Marie Branwell came from Penzance and her home in Chapel Street is now a Brontë shrine). There are ancient tumble-down stone walls in this area, and it seemed a good place in which to play with my metal detector.

'If you hold the trowel,' I said to Jeannie, 'I'll sweep the ground.'

I was now interrupted by the donkeys. They came thundering down the narrow path, Fred in the lead, and when they reached us they swerved to the right and into the entrance to the Brontë wood; and there they came to a full stop. I have a wire taut across the entrance. I had fixed it because the donkeys used to have a habit of entering the wood to gnaw at the bark of the trees. Thus they had to be banned from entering; and on this occasion they stood sulkily beside the wire, looking back at me and my metal detector, and Jeannie with the trowel in her hand.

I chose a spot to sweep which was close to a hawthorn, itself a donkey victim. Its bark also was gnawed, and the only way I was able to protect it was by winding wire round the trunk and branches so that donkey teeth met wire as well as bark.

I swept the grass-covered ground, swaying the disc of the detector to and fro . . . and there was silence. Then I looked up, and found the donkeys were watching me with fascination. What could he possibly be doing? I continued to sway. Then I looked towards the donkeys again, and saw that Fred, a very inquisitive looking Fred, had begun slowly to advance towards me.

Jeannie at this moment said: 'Sweep over closer to me.'

I moved over.

I swayed the disc slowly.

There was a banshee cry!

'I've got something!' I shouted, as if a trout had taken my fly. 'There, Jeannie, just where I'm holding it. Go on, dig!'

The donkeys stampeded.

Heads up, Fred making a weird banshee cry himself, they fled up the path we had come down. The sound of the metal detector had terrified them.

'At least,' I said, 'we can get on with the digging without interference.'

'You mean I can get on with the digging!'

Not for long.

Jeannie, on her knees, was scooping in the soil with her trowel when Fred, a fascinated Fred, came gingerly back. He came up to her, stood looking at her.

'Go away, Fred,' said Jeannie, giving him a push, then continuing her digging.

Fred had a habit which, an experienced donkey owner once told me, might break my neck. It was a loving gesture on his part, a gesture which took place when I sat on a rock or a hedge at donkey head level. I would be sitting there, and he would wander across, paw the ground at my feet, then stretch his head forward so that it rested on my head. His was a heavyweight head; and I can appreciate the warning.

'My wrist is tired,' said Jeannie, 'and my fingers can't grip any more.'

I took the trowel from her, and within a few minutes I was calling out I had found the object of the banshee howl. No false alarm this time. My metal detector had pinpointed the three-inch-deep rim of an ancient iron pot. My toy was justifying itself. I was able to say to Jeannie that I wasn't such a fool to buy it.

66

We left for the cottage after that, Jeannie holding the trophy, the donkeys following us; and when we reached the gate, the donkeys wanted to continue coming with us; and we told them they couldn't.

'You've twenty acres and a whole day to spend munching there,' said Jeannie.

Strange that some people would have disapproved of her speaking in that way. Strange that such people would feel it embarrassing. One of the great pleasures of life is to find someone who unties a knot in your mind, and so enables you to talk and feel without inhibitions. Even an animal can untie the knot.

I spent the remainder of the morning charging up and down the daffodil meadows bordering the coastal path, clinging to the handlebars of the Condor as it swathed the undergrowth. The meadows, however, did not contain fashionable daffodils. Once upon a time they fetched a good price – Sulphur, Actaea, California, King Alfred – but their popularity had faded; and we only continued to care for them in the hope that their popularity might one day return. Only one meadow retained its former glory, the little meadow beside the path containing Obvallaris, a miniature yellow daffodil; and we also have these in a few of the cliff meadows. Sometimes they take a rest for a year and blooms are scarce. When they bloom in profusion, we have a financial bonanza.

I roared the Condor back to the cottage, manoeuvred it

into the shelter beside the Leyland tractor, then went to join Jeannie. She greeted me with a glass of Rhine wine in her hand, knowing that I would be tired and would welcome it.

'Have you seen Cherry?' I asked.

There had been no sign of her at breakfast time. Indeed we had not seen her since the previous afternoon; and I found myself feeling concerned.

'No sign.'

'It's quite mild outside,' I said, 'let's take our drinks up to the bridge.'

'Half a moment, I'll put on a jersey.'

I went up to the bridge on my own, carrying my field glasses with me. I always have my field glasses at hand because there may be a ship or yacht or fishing boat I want to look at; or, at this particular time of year, I might suddenly see the first of the fieldfares, or there may be a day-light tawny owl hooting in the bare trees; or, as it proved to be on this occasion, a black cat to watch. Cherry.

Cherry was on the ledge of the stone wall between the apple tree and Jeannie's studio hut. I was relieved to see her. Her absence since the previous afternoon had made me impatient to see her again; and when I saw her on this stone ledge, I picked up my field glasses and focused them on her.

I am not clinically knowledgeable. I am one of those, Jeannie is like me, who find it an intrusion into a special privacy when the illnesses of public figures are disclosed to the world; and, for that matter, we are both in agreement about the filming of any operation which intrudes on the very personal privacy of a patient. The intrusion seems to reflect that morbid mood of the public which enjoys standing around watching the tragic results of a motorway accident.

The sun had come out to shine on Cherry, and I saw quite clearly a light-coloured line down her left side, as if fur had only recently begun to grow there.

And when Jeannie joined me, I gave her the field

glasses, and asked her what she thought was the cause.

'This is extraordinary,' she said, after a moment of looking, 'it looks as if she's been spayed.'

'That's what I think,' I said.

The following morning we called on our vet, and told him of our suspicions. He was pleasantly jovial.

'Tom cats in the neighbourhood will prove you right or wrong.'

Then he added more seriously. 'From what you tell me about the fur she must have been spayed about two months ago.'

Cherry, therefore, had belonged to somebody who had specially cared for her, somebody who must be pining for her at that very moment.

Where, where, had she come from?

It was now that Cherry truly began to be a part of our lives.

SIX

'I've learnt something about you today,' said Jeannie, 'that I didn't know before.'

'The secret of a happy marriage – the unexpected keeps it alive,' I replied.

Jeannie was holding a magazine in her hand.

'I've been in the confusion room,' she went on; the confusion room being where unwanted objects are deposited, where there are a pile of expendable books, where I write letters and deal with bills, and where 'Labour Warms', the cupboard which used to be in my nursery with its slogan 'Labour Warms, Sloth Harms', stores manuscripts and photographs dating back to my childhood. The confusion room is, in fact, the other half of the stables, and on the other side of the wall I sometimes listen to the shuffling feet of the donkeys. 'And,' continued Jeannie, 'I was looking through a drawer of Labour Warms, and found this.'

'What's this?'

'It's an article you wrote in your early twenties about your likes and dislikes.' Then she added: 'I never knew you put your anti-cat feelings into print.'

I remembered the article but not its contents. The article had a dramatic effect on my life. It was read by a newspaper proprietor who thereupon engaged me to write a highly-publicised newspaper column; and within a few weeks I was being treated like a present day pop star. Girls would rush up to my car when I was held up at traffic lights, my photograph careered around London on the tops of buses; and on one occasion when I visited the Hammersmith Palais, as it was then called, such was the rush at me that my accompanying photographer had to call out: 'Calm girls, calm!' It was a hilarious period.

'Well,' I said, 'I can't possibly remember what I wrote.'

'I'll remind you,' said Jeannie, 'about just one item in it.' And she had begun to laugh.

'Go on,' I said.

'You wrote,' and Jeannie was continuing to laugh, 'that among your dislikes there was one particular dislike . . . cats. You disliked cats,' you wrote, 'because they are so impersonal!'

'I was being honest at the time.'

A dubious note in my voice because I sensed what she was about to say.

'And look at you now! You get out of bed in the middle of the night to look for Ambrose if he's not indoors! And you have a stray cat which in a few weeks you'll be worrying about in the same way! Oh it's so funny how people can change!'

She was speaking the truth. It is funny. One can change one's views about people as one can about animals, and do so quite quickly sometimes.

'Anyhow,' I said churlishly, 'it was your fault. If I hadn't married you, I wouldn't have changed my mind.'

'But you did marry me,' said Jeannie.

'All right, all right, you win. I married you, and you changed my attitude towards cats. I'm delighted you did so.' I paused.

'Go on.'

'When I was a bachelor,' and it was now my turn to laugh, 'I was given some advice by the husband of a successful marriage. He told me that the one who won the first domestic victory in a marriage controlled the marriage from then on.'

'Converting you to be pro-cat meant I had the victory?'

'On the contrary, it shows up the flaw in the advice. We each had a victory. On the one hand you changed my attitude. On the other hand I proved you had a husband who was open-minded enough to listen to you!'

We were in the porch. The British Airways helicopter passed noisily by, though it was a thousand feet up and a mile off shore, on its way back from the Scilly Islands; it made such a noise because the cloud level was low.

'Look,' said Jeannie suddenly, 'look at what is staring at us on the rock beneath the water butt.'

There was Cherry.

'It's going to be Cherry's victory now,' said Jeannie, and I knew she was wryly amused in a kind way, 'not mine this time.'

'She's not won yet,' I said, 'she hasn't even entered the contest.'

'Not entered? Look what she's doing!'

Cherry was proceeding to perform the particular gesture which cats seem to believe is irresistible. It is the turnover gesture, the gesture which results in the display of silky fur undercarriage, spasmodic wriggling on the back, and pretty poses involving paws resembling baby fists. This bewitching behaviour often produces cries of admiration even from neutral observers; and such applause, after a minute or two, signals a changing course of action upon the part of the cat. Having bewitched, the cat will return to his normal routine. He will collect himself, maybe have a token wash, then stalk away. He has displayed his power over the human race to his satisfaction.

Cherry had chosen to perform the turnover gesture on a flat stone where Ambrose is sometimes fed when he wishes to have his meal out of doors instead of in; and the stone is below the small bird table which is wedged among small rocks, a canopy of fuschia above it. As I will tell, however, the days of this bird table were numbered.

Cherry, with her eye on us in the porch, quickly completed the first stage of her turnover gesture, and lay there wriggling, and displaying a feature of herself we had only partly observed before. From a distance, even from a few feet, she appeared to be all black, but now we were able to observe her in detail. There were flecks of ginger in her coat, and while two of her paws were jet black, a front one was cream with a narrow line of black in the centre, and a rear one had just a touch of cream. She had, too, a little shirt of cream but, as she lay wriggling, paws in the air as if she was kneading, it was her undercarriage that caused a cry of admiration from Jeannie. It was mostly black but a portion was the colour of apricot; and when she repeated the turn-over gesture a few days later I heard Jeannie call out: 'Come and look. Cherry is showing her apricots!'

Cherry had begun to infiltrate. The turnover gesture had been her first move. A second was soon to occur. By now she had been hovering around for nearly a month, exasperating Jeannie by sometimes absenting herself for twenty-four hours and more. Then she would reappear, and the time chosen was always about ten o'clock in the morning. It was the time when she had learnt to accept a breakfast, a time when Jeannie would be on the look out for her, a plate of Whiskas in her hand, ready to place the plate on the shelf of stones which surrounded a small flower bed beneath Annie's Folly. It was at this spot that Cherry's next move was executed.

Her habit was to eat from this plate, cover up what she left over with grass or any earthy debris, then skedaddle away. On the occasion of her next move, however, she stayed motionless on the shelf of stones. She stayed motionless until Jeannie, lured by this stillness, approached her, then touched her. Those who possess Jeannie's attitude towards cats will understand her excitement, while the rest of us tolerate it with amusement. For she greeted me when I saw her half an hour later with such joy that I thought the morning post must have brought us news of a financial bonanza.

'I touched her!' she exclaimed.

This response to pleasure on Jeannie's part, the naïvety of her excitement, was an example of her naturalness. Naïvety, however, can deceive. She is one of those people only fools underestimate.

The success of the incident encouraged Cherry to make a third move. It took place the following day at lunchtime when I was sitting in the chair in front of the fireplace, spreading Cambuzola on a piece of Jeannie's home-made bread, and listening to 'The World At One'. I glanced at the square window opposite which is set in a cavity of the two-feet-thick cottage wall, and saw Cherry eagerly looking in. It was a pretty sight which had additional charm because on the white-painted base of the cavity was a collection of china and glass ornaments that we had been given from time to time.

'Cherry is a cat in the window,' I called out to Jeannie. Jeannie was in the bedroom looking for a letter she had to answer.

'Come quick . . . Oh, she's gone!'

Perhaps she had been frightened by my voice; or just lost her nerve as she looked into the cottage. There was so much at stake. She wanted to infiltrate. She wanted a home.

She was soon to have a setback, and I was the cause of it. Her tactics – and I have seen similar tactics before, first by Lama, then by Oliver and Ambrose – were to win her way by appearing vulnerable; and I had, if I am true to myself, always been affected by such behaviour. A lost cat, a cat

74

about whom we had made such thorough enquiries to find whence she came, a hungry cat . . . I think it is understandable that I should develop, contrary to my reasoned thinking, an increasing interest in her.

Thus, when I myself found her one breakfast time staying motionless on the shelf of stones, an empty plate beside her, my reaction, like Jeannie, was to put out a hand and touch her.

Unfortunately I did not remain silent. I found myself cooing at her, making those soft burbling noises which I have so often despised when made by cat worshippers. I stretched out a finger and traced it up and down her little black head; and she responded by turning her head towards me, and producing what can only be described as a cat smile. The mouth moved so that I saw the little white teeth. No sound.

Sound, however, came from elsewhere. Sound came from the depths of the escallonia bush close by. It was a whining, unfriendly sound. It began in low key, then slowly rose in a crescendo. Too late I realised I had been caught *in flagrante delicto*, that my cooing noises had been overheard. Too late.

Ambrose leapt from the escallonia bush, caught Cherry off balance, bowled her over . . . and I thought there was going to be murder. There was no murder, no injury, just bruised feelings. Within a few seconds they had parted. Cherry fled, Ambrose glared. I was the object of the glaring, not the fleeing Cherry. I had betrayed him. But he did not prolong his anger. He had flared up because he believed himself unjustly provoked, and that was that as far as he was concerned. Soon afterwards he was rubbing himself, friendly fashion, against my leg.

Moreover, during the coming night, he displayed an affection for us which was special. Normally he would have chosen a place on the sofa where he would curl up and sleep, only jumping up on our bed when the dawn chill set in. On the evening after the breakfast time upset, he jumped up on our bed soon after lights out; and began to purr.

Ambrose has always been a great purrer. As a kitten he would break out in purrs for no apparent reason; and as he grew older and he and Oliver slept on the bed, pinioning us, neither able to move a leg until cramp agonisingly forced one of us to do so, he continued to be a great purrer. Such a great purrer that Oliver would sometimes, his own rest disturbed, give him a bash with a paw, as if he was saying to him: 'Shut up!'

On this particular evening, Ambrose comfortably placed on our bed, we both fell asleep almost at once. It is one of the special pleasures of living in a cottage far from other habitations and, most important, without possessing a telephone, that one can go to bed early without the possible threat of being disturbed. As a result I will often sleep solidly until three in the morning when I will probably wake up, and a wake period begins. On this occasion I once again woke up at three o'clock . . . A quiet night outside except for the hush noise of the sea, but inside on the bed, a roaring purr.

I have a digital clock on a chair beside my side of the bed, and after a few minutes I glanced at its flicking light and noted the time. It was five minutes past three. Ambrose was lying in elongated fashion across Jeannie. She was sound asleep. No knowledge of Ambrose's presence despite his weight. No knowledge of his purr.

I, on the other hand, lay there fantasising about situations past and future, the long-playing purr as background music . . . Half an hour, three-quarters of an hour, an hour, an hour and a quarter, an hour and a half. Without a moment's rest Ambrose continued to purr.

I wanted to share the situation with Jeannie, and I nudged her, and she woke up.

'Don't move,' I said quickly, 'lie absolutely still. Listen.'

'What's all this about?' she murmured.

I saw her move her arm.

'Don't touch him!'

'Have you gone mad?'

'Ambrose is in the process of winning a world record.'

76

'No, really. You wake me up and are talking absolute nonsense.'

'Quiet. I'll explain in a moment.'

Ambrose had stirred; and the engine driving the purr was slowing down. Then it stopped, and there was silence. I looked at the digital clock. The lights flickered to twenty minutes to five.

'One hour forty minutes at least!'

'What does that mean?'

'It means that Ambrose without anyone stroking him or putting their hand on him has purred non-stop all that time. Couldn't that be a world record?'

'You really are silly,' said Jeannie, though I reckoned that it was a kind of silliness which she enjoyed. 'Isn't he silly, Ambrose?'

His reply was to stretch, walk to the bottom of the bed, jump from there to the window sill, and out into the night.

Next morning at breakfast, as I tapped the top of a boiled egg, Jeannie asked: 'About that world record. What are you going to do about it?'

Ideas born of a three o'clock morning wake often fade by breakfast time.

'It seemed a good idea at the time,' I said doubtfully.

'You're not going to do anything about it? You're not going to write to the *Guinness Book of Records*?'

'Well,' I said, surrendering my enthusiasm of a few hours earlier, 'what would I say?'

'Just what happened.'

Jeannie had performed a takeover of my enthusiasm.

'Tell them of the rules you have formulated,' she went on, 'tell them that no one must touch a cat once the purring starts, and that the cat will be disqualified if this is done, just as a marathon runner would be disqualified if a motorist gave him a lift.'

'That's a bit much,' I said, 'comparing Ambrose's long-distance purr with a long-distance runner.'

'Go on,' said Jeannie, pushing me, 'do something. Write to the Guinness people. Get Ambrose in the record book!'

I never did write. But I often lie awake at three o'clock in the morning listening to Ambrose's purr, watching the digital clock, wondering whether he might be about to break the purring record of that first occasion. In my capacity as time-keeper I fluffed his chances a few nights ago. He had reached a time spell of one hour twenty minutes, the record seemed about to be broken . . . and I fell asleep.

Cherry was to prove that she also had a short memory, or perhaps she was telling me that she had a forgiving nature. Or perhaps she was being driven to forget and forgive, and pretend that Ambrose's attack had never taken place, because she knew this was her last chance. If she could not infiltrate Minack, there was nowhere else for her to go. If this attitude motivated her planning, she was on dangerous ground.

For instance, I remained obstinately protective of Ambrose. I did not approve of his attacking Cherry that morning when I stroked her with my finger, making foolish cooing noises; and yet, sad as I was that tranquillity was being disrupted, I understood his fury. He was a mirror of all of us who see our citadel threatened. It may be a physical citadel, a home in which one has lived so long that it seems to you as permanent as the rocks facing the sea; and then an envelope is slipped through the letterbox, and when you open it there is the jargon telling you that your world will soon be over. Or it may be an emotional citadel – a special relationship that is being threatened, a love affair is ended. Whatever the citadel that is in danger, it is understandable there is a desire to fight back.

Ambrose, intuitively, probably felt the same way towards Cherry. After all when first he came to Minack, he and Oliver were on the way to ousting Lama. Cherry, he might think, had a similar intention. For although age, in conventional terms, is the adding up of years passed, in realistic terms it depends upon an attitude of mind. Absurd, one might say, to relate a human condition to that of an animal. But why not? Human behaviour in many spheres today is so sickening that it is a wonder that we can maintain this sense of superiority over animals; a superiority which defends itself by alleging that animals, domestic animals in particular, do not have emotions like human beings. Ambrose, for instance, was growing old, but he still, in his own mind, was young.

Cherry's short memory, or forgiving nature, or more likely a determined one, resulted in her spending a night on a chair in the porch. I had forgotten to shut one of the case-ment windows, and it was ajar on a hook, and she had slipped through; and when in the morning I opened the sitting room door, I found her comfortably curled on a yellow cushion.

She surprised me by not moving. She blinked at me, then quivered her mouth, displaying little white teeth. She seemed to be luring me towards her. I was aware, however, that Ambrose was somewhere behind me in the sitting room, and I was not going to be caught out again. Thus I refused to be lured. Instead, like a schoolmaster, I felt I had to impose my authority. I spoke to her harshly.

'What do you think you are doing there?' I said.

This promptly resulted in Cherry fleeing from the cushion, and disappearing outside; and I returned to the sitting room.

'That was my fault,' I said to Jeannie. 'I'll remember to shut the window in future.'

But I did not remember. I deliberately did not remember. From then on the casement window was left ajar for Cherry to enter.

'Derek,' said Jeannie, when she realised this, 'you say one thing, then act another. You are so full of opposites.'

'You too,' I replied.

Most of us are full of opposites. Jeannie, for instance, revelled in her time as publicity officer of the Savoy Hotel Group, where she was described by an American magazine as 'the prettiest publicity girl in the world', and yet she equally revelled in isolating herself in a Cornish cottage.

She once received a telegram from the BBC asking her to appear on a late-night television programme in which she had to give her views on a television series based on Arnold Bennett's *Imperial Palace*. It was at the height of the daffodil season. One day she was bent double picking daffodils in the rain, the next she was being fêted in London; and she enjoyed both days. The truth is that emotional experiences are as unpredictable as a changing sea, and there are no rules to govern them.

Educational policy, however, aims to make people believe that such rules can be created through knowledge. No account is taken of intuition. Drench knowledge into the young is the policy, force them into the examination rat race and frighten them into believing that failure will deny them a happy future. Yet this cramming of knowledge can create a kind of straightjacket in the way one thinks. One tries to remember, in a crisis, what is in the rule book rather than relying on instant intuition. Art and literature is also often influenced by such a straightjacket. A promising artist may be so drilled into obeying the instructions of the art teacher that spontaneity is lost. Or a tutor, compelled by examination edict, will insist that a book should be studied with such clinical attention that any enjoyment of the book is banished.

A pity there are no Professors of Common Sense at universities. They might help to balance this pursuit of knowledge. Common sense will have far more influence on the lives of the majority than knowledge crammed into their minds for the sake of examination results. Common sense is a constant companion. Common sense can often identify the base of a complicated problem which is denied to brilliant professional thinkers. Common sense can steer the future of failed school-leavers. The possession of common sense is an asset which will always prevail.

The rains came, day after day, in the second half of November, and I was annoyed with myself that I had been lulled by the first half. There was so much to do outside that I should have done. Instead I had been seduced into inaction. The weather was soft like a balmy spring and I had preferred to meander rather than work, promising myself that on the morrow I would take out my brush cutter and finish cutting down the cliff meadows, or shovel out the ditch beside the lane, or check the gutters, or plug with polythene any gap in the greenhouses where the glass had been broken. These are the sort of tasks I should have done before winter came full upon us, but I had preferred to stroll on Oliver land with the donkeys, sit on the rocks joining sleepy gulls, and pretend I was on holiday.

Thus I felt guilty and thwarted when the rains came. The lane, ditch uncleared, became like a river-bed. The gutters, unblocked, spilt their contents. The undergrowth of the cliff meadows was drowned into a matty flatness. A lesson to be learnt which I will never learn is to seize the kind weather, for the harsh will soon follow.

Ambrose did not mind. He created a series of beds in the hay in the Orlyt, round circles, and he moved from one to the other according to his whim of the day. Fred and Merlin stood lugubriously, ignoring the comfort of the stables, or was it only Fred who preferred to look miserable? Fred was a gypsy conceived in the hills of Connemara. He was bred to face the weather in all its conditions. Merlin, on the other hand, was a thoroughbred. I am sure he would have stayed indoors had it not been for Fred's insistence on going outside.

The gulls were unperturbed. Knocker still knocked. Philip still arrived twice a day to squawk. As for Cherry, she found new places in which to shelter. She found a large crack underneath the rock where Philip liked to stand and squawk; and she found the bird table.

The bird table, as I have said, was wedged among small rocks with a canopy of fuschia above it; and it was placed within a few feet of the porch door. I hated seeing Cherry hiding there. The bird table was there for the regulars, Charlie and Shelagh the chaffinches, the blue tits and the tom tits, and the dim little dunnocks. I could go out in my bedroom slippers whatever the weather and leave on it a handful of crumbs or, more popular, a handful of sunflower seeds. Cherry, after she became a squatter, denied me this. She denied too the chance of these little birds enjoying these handfuls in the dry. I had to place them elsewhere, and on stones where the rain soaked them. Cherry, at this stage, was not gaining popularity with me.

The rains clouded the views, and for two or three days on end I might say to Jeannie that Carn Barges had remained hidden. It didn't matter to us. There is an exquisite pleasure in feeling isolated. There is a sense of such joy. Clouds physically helping one to shut one's mind. No telephone to jangle one. There is for a while the sweet illusion that one is immune from the stresses of the outside world.

The first Christmas cards, the first Christmas letters had already begun to arrive; and on receiving them I felt admiration for those who were able to organise their Christmas greetings so far in advance. Jeannie and I try to do so but always fail. We start thinking, for instance, in late summer, as to what kind of Christmas card we should have, and then we delay a decision, and we get into a panic. Shall it be a photograph or a drawing? And how many should we order?

One evening we had decided, while Ambrose slept comfortably in a corner of the sofa and Cherry, rain in cascades around her, was curled on the bird table, that our Christmas card of the year should be a photograph I had taken of Jeannie, one hot August morning, carrying a hoe in the garden. I was more in favour of it than Jeannie was. She hates her photographs.

'We're late with it,' said Jeannie.

'We're always late. We'll just have to push the photographic shop to produce the cards more quickly.'

A day or two after this conversation, I had a letter which vividly brought back to me the day on which this photograph of Jeannie was taken. Such a lovely, sunny day, and because the sun shines on the cottage from the direction of the Lizard in the morning, I had seized the opportunity to pose Jeannie against the background of the cottage, the flowers of the rockery around her.

Later that morning we had to dress up in formal fashion because we had a function to attend in the early afternoon. We were dressed, about to enter the Volvo, when a car drew up opposite the cherry tree. The driver, a young woman, got out, then went round to the passenger's door, and I could see that she was helping a child who seemed to be in some difficulty. The child was about six, and I saw that she was struggling because she was wearing calipers, thus restraining the spontaneous movement of her legs.

Suddenly the child saw Fred.

Fred had emerged from inside the stables, and he was stretching his neck over the wooden fence, pushing out his head towards the child as if in welcome. The child, in her excitement, freed herself from the calipers, and walked unaided up to him.

Her mother has never forgotten the magic of that moment, as Jeannie and I have never forgotten; and the letter recalled for us that summer day, brought us up to date, and filled us with wonder at the courage of children.

The child had endured periods in hospital and a series of operations; and all the while, her mother said in the letter, the child had clung to her memory of Fred. Fred had become a talisman for the future.

'Do you know what she longs to do?' wrote her mother. 'One Christmas, when she is better, she wants to spend Christmas Eve with Fred and Merlin in the stables.'

Jeannie and I were to have the child in our minds as we stood in the stables on Christmas Eve, listening to the donkeys munching mince pies.

SEVEN

Cherry changed her tactics after Christmas. She became bolder. On New Year's day, for instance, I found her in the afternoon curled up on the sofa. How had she got there? Jeannie and I had been for a stroll up the lane with Ambrose, and we had shut the front door, and the bedroom window which we sometimes leave open was also shut.

'Cherry!' I said. 'What are you doing here?'

A glance at me, a leap to the floor, and she was away across the room towards the spare bedroom and the bathroom. It was through the narrow opening of the bathroom window that she had entered the cottage.

The following morning she was indoors again; and this time she was warming herself in the chair opposite the log fire. This is the chair where Jeannie generally sits, and where Ambrose often sits on her lap, purring contentedly while she combs him; and it was Jeannie who found her there.

Jeannie was more gentle than I had been. She did not speak loudly. As a result she was rewarded, according to her own way of looking at the incident, with a minor triumph. She picked up Cherry who made an effort to struggle, sat herself down in the chair holding Cherry on her lap, and for half a minute listened to a suspicion of a purr.

Only for half a minute. The bedroom window had been

left ajar; and Jeannie suddenly saw Ambrose a few feet away on the carpet, balefully glaring at her. She reacted almost in panic. She clasped Cherry round her middle, hurried with her to the bedroom window, and pushed her into the garden. She then returned to placate Ambrose. It was achieved by a saucer of freshly-cooked coley.

In certain circumstances this developing cat conflict might have been amusing. We all like diversions in our lives, incidents that in cricketing terms can be described as a change of bowling. But in this case I was not amused. I could cope, reluctantly, with the tension that had been created outside the cottage, the sudden scream when one cat met the other, but I could not bear the prospect of coping with a similar tension indoors. I was uptight enough about personal problems without adding cat ones to them.

Jeannie and I, for instance, were trying to formulate plans which would help to exploit our activities. It sounds idyllic to be living a life which is free from nine-to-five work; and where you are free from office politics. Yet, as a consequence, you have to face other kinds of problems. You may be free, but you still have to earn a living; and if you have chosen to be producers you have to sell your products. In our case the products consisted of daffodils, and words.

We were, therefore, dependent on marketing people who were immersed in selling a multitude of similar products; and we were inclined to expect too much of such people. This is, of course, a common mistake which is made by anyone who is consumed by a personal problem. That problem, to the person concerned, is unique. The person has spent so many of his waking hours thinking and talking about it that he is convinced that everyone is equally interested in the problem.

Our problem, and the way we were trying to deal with it is not, however, so easily explained. Our problem was to find ways of putting over ideas to the marketing people which would help to sell our products.

We had, for instance, a belief that when someone buys a bunch of daffodils it would enhance their pleasure if it was known where the daffodils had been grown. A daffodil, for instance, grown in a Cornish cliff meadow close to the sea, and for sale in a shop at the beginning of February, is a more romantic flower than a daffodil grown in a factory-style Lincolnshire greenhouse.

Hence Jeannie and I had cards printed explaining where our daffodils came from; and we put a card in every box we sent to Covent Garden. Our wholesaler at Covent Garden was enthusiastic. In the vast area of Covent Garden anonymity, a personal touch had been introduced. Not so the retailers, except for one of them. The rest showed no interest whatsoever in our idea to make a bunch of daffodils a romantic affair.

'They couldn't care less,' our friend at the wholesalers told us. 'A daffodil is just a daffodil.'

It was this lack of imagination on the part of marketing people that was our problem, and which made us feel so frustrated. Jeannie and I would develop an idea, put it forward, and nothing would come of it. We would think up another idea. We would spend hours writing a letter describing the idea, changing it several times, then changing it yet again; and then waking up in the middle of the night, thinking again about the letter, so alert that the prospect of sleep was far away, suddenly thinking of a new phrase to insert into the letter, angry too that such mental effort was necessary to put over an idea which would be of pecuniary benefit both to the marketing people and ourselves; and then in the morning I would hopefully type out the letter which had given so much trouble.

'It is such a good letter,' Jeannie would say encouragingly as I put it into the envelope and stuck on the stamp.

The period of waiting for a reply had begun. Like that of waiting for the result of an examination, or of an application for a job. A vacuum time, but tense.

Sometimes we were pleased with the reply, sometimes dispirited, sometimes angry. There were the occasions when the sender showed understanding and enthusiasm, and we would open a bottle of wine to celebrate. There were other occasions when it was obvious that the sender had no vibes for us and had little interest in our product or knowledge of our background. It was then that our anger would rise because we realised all our efforts would be wasted by poor marketing. On such occasions, tempted as I was to unleash my anger by writing a torrid reply, I kept myself in check by remembering what my mother used to do in similar circumstances.

My mother would retire to her bedroom when she was enraged by someone, but aware that it would be unwise to make her feelings public; and in her bedroom she would write a furious letter to the person concerned, proceed to read it aloud to herself several times, then tear it up. I remember one school holiday when a friend of my mother's came to stay for a few days. My mother was a delightful hostess but she believed firmly in short-staying guests. Unfortunately on the third day of her friend's stay the lady fell over the dog she had brought with her, and broke her ankle. Hence, instead of days, the friend stayed for six weeks. My mother was daily in her bedroom writing furious letters.

I was in the mood for writing such a letter that day when the tension between Ambrose and Cherry had moved indoors. I was sitting at my desk ruminating about it, and Jeannie was at the other end of the room, standing, her back to the log fire. She looked so young and pretty, slim in her grey slacks, her head and dark hair on the level of the lintel behind her.

'You know,' she said, 'our feeling of frustration is a common disease. It is there everywhere in one form or another, in personal relationships, in committee rooms, in businesses, everywhere. So we're lucky to have it on such a small scale. The trouble with us is that we are probably too subtle. We rely too much on expecting people to respond to us by intuition.'

'The sweet pleasure of unspoken understanding.'

'Yes.'

'What shall we do then?'

'Let's make a New Year resolution to stop worrying over a matter we can't do anything about.'

'You have a point . . . We can worry about something else.'

Jeannie laughed.

'What do you mean?'

'We can worry about resolving the cat conflict instead.'

'More rewarding.'

'Even more difficult. Nothing on earth will let me have Ambrose upset.'

'Of course not.'

'If that is the case, I have a proposal to make.'

I had been making notes of my idea for a few days, and they were in front of me on my desk.

'If Cherry is to stay permanently with us,' I now explained, 'I believe she ought to pass an examination, something which I will call "C Levels".'

'Poor Cherry, don't make it too hard for her.'

'What I have in mind,' I went on, 'is that if she doesn't pass the tests, we'll get rid of her.'

'Derek,' Jeannie said, sounding alarmed, 'you can't mean it!'

'Yes I do,' I said firmly, 'if she doesn't fit in with our way of living she's out.'

'You sound like a nineteenth-century headmaster, right out of *Tom Brown's Schooldays*,' Jeannie said. Then she added doubtfully: 'What are these C Levels she has to pass?'

I looked at my notes.

'There are nine C Levels,' I said.

'Nine? As many as that? Are you asking her to pass all of them? And what are they?'

'Out of the nine,' I said, and I sounded very serious, 'Cherry will have to pass five of them. That doesn't sound harsh, does it?'

'That depends on the C Levels. What are they?'

I proceeded to read them out. This was the list.

1. She must not catch birds.
2. She must be house clean.
3. She must not show interest in food on the dining room table.
4. No rotovating of the carpet with her claws.
5. No digging up of plants in the garden.
6. Must not be too friendly with strangers.
7. Must never wander far.
8. No bringing into the cottage of live mice or rabbits.
9. She must not cause us anxiety at night by hiding when she is called.

'There you are,' I said, 'these are her C Levels, and I propose that we should judge the result on the anniversary of her coming here. If she passes she's here for good.'

Jeannie looked at me in astonishment.

'You're not serious . . . The anniversary is nine months away!'

'Well,' I said, hedging, 'the first two on the list are the essential ones. We can be liberal in our attitude towards the other ones.'

'Poor Cherry, and she won't know what is being expected of her.'

'I could have added another C Level to the list – she must not annoy Ambrose. But I didn't because I fear that would have been impossible for her to pass. She's certain to annoy him. She does so already. Ambrose's life is never going to be the same now that she is infiltrating indoors.'

I was not, of course, feeling as stern as I sounded. I knew in my heart that I would be pleased if Cherry passed her C Levels. I just wanted to be careful. I was aware that certain cat characteristics were responsible for my one-time anti-cat attitude, and so I was on guard. By proposing conditions, therefore, I felt I had taken out an insurance. If Cherry was to prove to be an unpleasant cat, I was now free to get rid of her, find her another home; and Ambrose would then be able to resume his leisurely ways.

Up to this moment Cherry had been found only twice

indoors, the first time by me on the sofa, the second time by Jeannie in the chair in front of the fire. There was soon to be a third time. Late at night I found her curled up in a ball on the bed in the spare room. She was startled by the light I had switched on, and with one leap she was in the bathroom and, just as on that first time, out through the gap of the partially-opened window.

This incident caused Jeannie and myself some concern. We realised that Cherry had now given up her outside sleeping quarters, and she had given them up for a very good reason. Wintry weather covered the region, a bitter east wind and frost-filled nights; and no cat would choose to sleep outside if it knew of a warm niche indoors. So what arrangements could we make for Cherry?

The bathroom window was normally kept shut, for Ambrose used our bedroom window as an exit and entrance. Cherry could not be expected to use it also, for she would have to pass within inches of Ambrose as he lay on our bed; and, in any case, at this stage, I would have hated it if she had done so. Nor would she have wanted to. She was scared of Ambrose. She, a very small, dainty cat, could be destroyed by Ambrose if he so decided. He was powerful, had killed a stoat and numerous large rabbits. Cherry was no match for Ambrose if she incurred his wrath. Hence the concern of Jeannie and myself now that Cherry was wanting to find shelter indoors at night. We might be able to act as peacemakers during the day, but not at night while we were asleep.

We therefore came to the conclusion we had to sacrifice some of our personal comfort if we were to solve the problem. We had, for instance, to keep the window of the bathroom ajar all night despite the fact we would be greeted by a freezing cold bathroom each morning. This was not all we had to do. Naturally we had to keep the sliding door dividing the spare bedroom from the sitting room shut at night to stop the cold draughts freezing the whole cottage, but there was also a hazard in connection with our conclusion which affected Cherry's entrance and exit methods.

The bathroom window, a casement window, faced the donkey field. Between the end of the bathroom and the field was a gap of about three feet. On the right side of the bathroom end were kept the two calor gas cylinders which heated the bath water. In front of the window itself was the three-foot gap between it and the field. Cherry, therefore, had to jump this gap; and it seemed to me to be a difficult jump even for a cat because the field side was higher than the window, and the window itself had only an inch-wide sill. Thus Cherry had to jump downwards, when she was entering the cottage, then on to the narrow sill and through the narrowly-opened casement window. She could easily hit her head against the glass if she misjudged the distance.

Why was I so concerned? I have no rational explanation. Jeannie looked at me as I outlined this concern, shrugged her shoulders, and said she didn't understand me.

'You chop and change so much,' and she was laughing. 'One moment you're talking as if you want to get rid of Cherry, the next you're worrying she might hit her head against the window.'

I knew, despite her comments, that Jeannie understood my attitude; and she was helpful when I said that I remembered we had somewhere a discarded ironing board which I thought would solve Cherry's jump problem. It was an absurd idea of mine, but Jeannie did not question its absurdity; and she found the discarded ironing board for me.

I placed it, wedged it would be a more accurate description, in the gap between window and field so that it acted as a form of bridge. Cherry's entrance and exit was now secure. Another stage in Cherry's infiltration into our lives had been successfully completed.

A few days later the calor gas delivery man arrived with a new calor gas cylinder.

'I don't want to be inquisitive,' he said, as he manoeuvred the cylinder into position, 'but what is an ironing board doing here?'

The spare room is, in fact, Jeannie's dressing room; and is the converted chicken house which we bought for £50 when first we came to Minack. At that time there was, of course, no bathroom attached, and we used the chicken house for bunching violets; and for Jeannie to write her book *Meet Me at the Savoy*. Then we decided to turn it into a bedroom – this again was before a bathroom was built on – and that decision has left us with a hefty piece of furniture we will never be able to remove unless we saw it apart.

It is a ceiling-high Victorian hall cupboard painted white, with sliding doors which stick. It was given us by Jeannie's parents in those first days when we were thankful to be given any kind of furniture. It came from a cottage they once owned in the country, and was used for overcoats and mackintoshes and boots. There is a different use for it today. It holds Jeannie's array of dresses.

The chicken house is now lined with hardboard which is covered by a pretty Werner Graaf wallpaper called 'Spring'. There are pictures on the walls, one of Monty curled asleep which Jeannie painted when we lived in the cottage overlooking the finish of the Boat Race at Mortlake; and it is uncanny to look at this picture, then at Ambrose, the double of Monty, when he too is curled asleep on the bed beneath it. There are other pictures, a drawing by Jeannie of Fred and Penny grazing in the QE2 field; and there is a beautiful example of needlework in colour of Ambrose on his rock, given us by a friend; and there is, in contrast, an unusual picture of a long-ago London hotel world, a caricature collection of the famous restaurateurs of the time.

We first saw this picture hanging on the wall of a small restaurant in Truro called the Rendezvous des Gourmets, a restaurant which, despite its size, was to win top awards as being one of the finest in the United Kingdom. We had first met its proprietor one Sunday afternoon when I looked out of the window and saw a little man standing by himself in the space opposite the cherry-tree. I went out to see him and he greeted me by saying: 'I've come to see Miss Nicol. Is she available? Would you tell her that Solomito is here who was once the personal waiter to the late Sir George Reeves-Smith.'

Miss Nicol, her maiden name, is how Jeannie was known when she handled the publicity affairs of the Savoy Hotel Group; and countless times since I have heard people, hotel people, call her Miss Nicol. Perhaps it was her youthfulness which captured the imagination of the hotel world who knew her; and now, years later, the legend of her time at the Savoy, the Berkeley and Claridge's persists. When we were dining at the Savoy recently, a wine waiter came to our table: 'Ah, Miss Nicol, I bring your favourite crème de menthe frappé – and with my compliments.'

Solomito was one of those who considered her a legend; and that afternoon when I saw him beside the cherry tree he had come to tell her about the Rendezvous des Gourmets; and how it was just an ordinary café when he bought it, and how his ambition was to make it one of the most famous restaurants in the country. Jeannie was naturally intrigued. She was aware of Solomito's background. Sir George Reeves-Smith was for many years the managing director of the Savoy Group, and he was the model for the hero of Arnold Bennett's *Imperial Palace*. He was a man known for his meticulous insistence on a high standard of service. Solomito, as his one-time personal waiter, had an equally high standard in his restaurant.

But today, this restaurant which was selected as one of

the six best in Britain, no longer exists. Solomito, having achieved his ambition, having seen his two pretty daughters educated, sold the restaurant; and then he and his wife, who was the genius in the kitchen, set off for the West Indies where he always wanted to live. The restaurant faded into obscurity.

When he left, Solomito gave Jeannie this picture which hangs on the wall in the spare room, a caricature collection of restaurateurs. It had hung in the room at the restaurant where people first had drinks, and Jeannie had always been interested in it.

I had known three of those caricatured in the picture. Maurice of the Trocadero, for instance, I knew as a school-boy. My aunt used to take me to the Trocadero during the weekend of the Eton and Harrow match at Lords. We used to go there after the theatre, and then we returned to her home at Bushey Heath by the last Greenline bus of the night. Quaglino I knew because I used to go to his restaurant with a young actress for a brief meal before she went to her theatre. The restaurateur I knew best, however, was Ferraro of the Berkeley. I was a clerk in Unilever when I first knew him; and I was always broke. Broke I may have been but I still wanted to take girls out in the evening; and in this respect Ferraro would come to my aid. He would let me take the girl to a corner table out of sight of the dance floor but where we could listen to the music. We would eat and drink very sparingly and then find that Ferraro had given us the evening free.

A restaurateur, by his manner, can break or make an occasion. Tycoons, knowing this, require to be flattered by his attention, and a love affair can be nurtured by his charm towards a couple. His aim is to boost egos, and make shy people more confident in themselves. The conventional method of achieving this is to be suave and solicitous, as used by most of the restaurateurs that Jeannie and I have known. There was one, however, and he was the most celebrated restaurateur of them all, who would often defy this convention. He was Luigi Donzelli, for many years at the Savoy Grill, then at Claridge's; and Jeannie can describe a thousand times when she has watched him greet the great names of the day who, in their turn, seemed to be honoured by the way he was greeting them.

Yet there would be occasions when he might appear to an outsider to have behaved abominably. Suddenly he would say to a well-known lady: 'Your dress today, the colour does not suit you. Last week the green made you so young and pretty!' This chauvinistic aggressiveness attracted women. The more so when, a few days later, he would come to them, wave his hands: 'Ah, today you look divine!'

Bruno, the present restaurateur of Claridge's Restaurant, says that a restaurateur must be like a theatrical producer. He must create a special atmosphere, a feeling of excitement, yet such excitement in an establishment of quality must be subdued. Luigi Donzelli certainly produced such excitement; and it was at the Savoy Grill, after first nights when the stars arrived for supper, that one was specially aware of his charisma. A small man with silver grey hair, a mischievous smile, always giving the impression of elegance, I would watch him on these occasions as he greeted the arrivals, then led them to their tables, each arrival being made to feel that they were the only ones that Luigi wanted to greet. Jeannie knew him from her first days at the Savoy. He always made a fuss of her, always arranged that she should have the best table, seeing that flowers were always there, and advising her on the choicest items on the menu, always done with a flourish. Jeannie that day was the only one he wanted to please, Jeannie and her guests.

He was far from our thoughts one summer Sunday when we had spent the morning picking tomatoes, weighing and packing them for the Monday market. Our hands had the green film which comes with picking tomatoes, and our clothes were dishevelled, and we were both in the mood of not wanting to see anyone at all. We were also a little depressed because we had a poor lunch to look forward to. We were ready, after our work, for an elegant lunch, a worthy lunch to celebrate all the hard work we had done.

But we only had a piece of Cheddar cheese, though of course we had our tomatoes to go with it, and home-made bread. Nonetheless Jeannie, who had no reason to be so, was apologetic. 'I'm sorry,' she said, 'I ought to have planned better. I didn't think we would eat all that chicken last night.' Then she added: 'Thank goodness we're alone.'

At that moment I happened to look out of the window; and I saw a man leaning over the fence in front of the cherry tree, talking to Fred who was pushing his nose at him. The back view seemed familiar. The man was impeccably dressed in the kind of casual clothes which you see advertised in expensive monthly magazines. He suddenly turned round, and looked towards the cottage.

'Good heavens, Jeannie,' I called out, 'a surprise special visitor . . . Out there talking to Fred is Luigi Donzelli!'

The unexpected guest. Nothing in the larder. Panic.

But Luigi, an hour later, sitting at the white iron-wrought table on the bridge, looking out upon the sweep of blue sea, was to say as he had Cheddar cheese, a bottle of Settesoli, tomatoes and home-made bread: 'This is a banquet!'

Snow came in the middle of January, falling overnight so that when we woke up and looked out from our pillows towards Monty's Leap, we saw a white lane instead of grey chippings; and all around, on the barn roof, on the Orlyt, on the bushes and trees lining the lane, was such an abundance of snow that we knew we were isolated.

It gave us a delicious feeling of freedom. There would be no post containing letters which might annoy us. Outdoor tasks which ought to be done could not be done. We were as isolated as if we were on a mountain peak – no cars could reach us, and as we have no telephone no message could disturb us. True, if we wanted to make the effort, we could force our way up the lane on foot to see our friends Jack and Alice Cockram and Mary and Mike Nicholls in the farmhouse at the top of the hill, but only a special emergency would make us do that. Meanwhile, without any sense of the guilt which seems to haunt one whenever one does something pleasurable outside the normal routine of one's life, we were ready to relax, like those in a school who have been given an unexpected day off. We were going to enjoy ourselves.

There were, however, Fred and Merlin, Ambrose and Cherry, and the birds. If we were enjoying ourselves, would they be doing so too? We were doubtful, very doubtful. We were so doubtful that, lying in bed with a second cup of tea, we began to worry.

'There's Ambrose, I'm worried about Ambrose,' Jeannie said. 'You know how in the past he's gone potty when there's snow, running away and hiding.'

'And what about Cherry?' I said. 'She's never seen snow . . . And supposing she gets caught up in a drift, how will we find her? She's never miaowed. We would never know where she was.'

Cherry indeed seemed to be a miaow-less cat. She seemed to be incapable of miaowing. At the moment when one would have expected her to miaow, she only opened a tiny slit of her mouth, displaying a row of little white teeth. No sound. Complete silence.

Thus we had two animals of complete silence. First Merlin, now Cherry. Merlin was the harder to understand because he would be standing by Fred while Fred was bellowing away; and I would have thought such bellowing would be infectious. I could not understand why Merlin should remain dumb. Were not donkeys renowned for their hee-haws?

One day, however, he was to hee-haw, an anguished cry of a hee-haw; and of that I will tell later. Meanwhile he was a silent donkey, just as Cherry was a silent cat.

I had got out of bed, and was by the window.

'Jeannie,' I said, 'the donkeys!'

'What do you mean?'

'They're out in the stable meadow!'

'What are they doing?'

'They're upside down, legs in the air, having a bath in the snow!'

EIGHT

We were therefore marooned. It would mean the daffodil harvest would be late. We normally began picking those in the bottom cliff meadows by the end of January; and sometimes when I have picked the first bunch, Jeannie has packed the first box, and we have taken it to be loaded on the lorry for Covent Garden, we have wondered where that first bunch had ended its journey. Who was the person who bought it? Where was the room it stood in a vase?

There was a deep drift of snow outside the porch door, and I was only able to push the door ajar. I then made it wider with my hands, throwing away the snow as if I was throwing away snowballs. As I was doing so there was a talkative cat noise behind; it was Ambrose telling me he wanted to go out after a cosy night indoors.

Our experience of Ambrose in snowtime was not going to be repeated. It is a crisis moment in the life of any cat person when their cat disappears, when it overstays its normal routine absence, and they are left, hour after hour, wondering what may have happened. True, the return, when it does take place, provides the cat person with hysterical happiness and a consequent special reward for the cat which has caused all the trouble . . . But there is always the threat that, this time, there might be no return. We were not going to risk Ambrose causing us such worry. Thus I told him he had to wait until I put on my Wellington boots; and then I would carry him down to the Orlyt where he could spend the day out of the snow-covered land – and with the door shut.

Cherry, surprisingly, was not to cause a problem. She had changed her tactics just in time. She now had a niche in the cottage. She had her own back door through the bathroom window. She was accepted by us as a resident; and she had already achieved that subtle accolade appreciated by discerning night-wandering cats of having their names anxiously called in the middle of the night, when the caller could have remained snugly in bed.

The occasion, of course, was before the snow arrived. I had woken up at two in the morning, and lay awhile in bed until the niggling wish to find out if Cherry was indoors made me get up and go to look. I slid out of bed, leaving Ambrose lying across a sleeping Jeannie close to her face, picked up a torch, and went through the rooms. No Cherry.

I thereupon decided that I had better go outside into the night and look for her. At that hour one has imaginative worries which have no substance in the morning. For instance, the first place I looked for her was at the waterbutt in case the top had fallen in, and Cherry with it. Then I walked down the lane, in dressing gown and slippers, to Monty's Leap where the stream was in full, winter flow, wondering whether she might have fallen in that too. And all the time I was calling: 'Cherry! Cherry!'

The lights were on in the cottage when I returned. Jeannie had woken up, heard my distant cries, and was now ready to join me.

'Are you sure,' she first said, 'that you have looked everywhere in the cottage that she could be?'

'All the usual places,' I replied.

But we were to find her indoors. While I was walking around the chilly outside, she was curled in a black ball on the cupboard shelf where my jerseys are kept.

There could be no false alarms during snowtime. Thus we closed the bathroom window entrance, organised a box, and told her she would have to stay indoors, as if she were in a town flat, until the snow had thawed; and fortunately she seemed quite happy to obey.

Indeed her readiness to co-operate set us again wondering as to where she came from. Her co-operation suggested she was perhaps a town cat who had escaped in some fashion to the country. Ambrose, on the other hand, being born of farm cat antecedents, was ready to be outside in any weather. Cherry, quite obviously, was not; and under this new snowtime regime she proceeded to find a corner in the cottage which, hopefully, would not result in a confrontation with Ambrose. It was well out of sight of Ambrose's normal evening quarters on the sofa in front of the fire. It was situated on the floor behind the chair where I sit at my Regency desk, between the bookcase and the storage heater. She was happy there all day, and all night. She at one end of the sitting room, Ambrose at the other until, at some stage of the night, Ambrose decided it was time to move to our bed, and transpose his person to Jeannie's shoulders or my legs.

Cats looked after, donkeys happy, small birds fed with

sunflower seeds, the gulls with bread – we could now consider ourselves.

'Jeannie,' I said, half way through that first morning, 'I have a plan.'

'What sort of plan?'

'Well,' I said, 'to get the most out of this isolation let's not listen to the news, radio or television.'

She laughed.

'I don't call that a plan! More like fulfilling a Walter Mitty dream!'

There is too much news. Past inhabitants of our cottage heard the news of Queen Anne's death, the American War of Independence, Queen Victoria's accession, without being cluttered by a multitude of subsidiary news. News that came to them was basic, never manufactured, never bearing the influence of political or commercial interests.

But today people are hypnotised by a well-groomed lady or gentleman staring at them while announcing a daily catalogue of woes. The pound is up, disaster for exports; the pound is down, disaster for imports. A picture comes on the screen of rows of Stock Exchange gentlemen frantically trying to obey the computers on their desks. Another picture appears of a bomb-blasted street in Northern Ireland. Another of violence in some African state. We stare back mindlessly at the announcer, watch the lips moving, then wait for the hovering smile which will accompany the inevitable closing item – a jokey item to counter the catalogue of woes.

'Of course,' I said, 'we'll have to keep in touch with the weather forecast.'

'Very practical.'

'We'll use Oracle or Ceefax, and we can always check if some serious news has happened.'

'The Walter Mitty dream is fading!'

'No, not fading. What I have in mind is to stop looking at faces and hearing voices.'

'Oh, I see what you mean.'

The value of Oracle or Ceefax is that you are able to

select the news you are interested in. Page number 101 gives a summary of the news which is kept up to date throughout the day. If an item is of interest you press the buttons on your hand control to achieve the appropriate page number; and a straightforward account of the item concerned will then appear on the screen. If you want the weather forecast, local or nationwide, the same method applies. The charm of this news service is that there are no embellishments. It provides facts. No striving after sensation, no hype, no fear of manufactured news as so often happens in newspapers. It amuses me, as a one-time newspaperman myself, to observe journalists getting very excited about defending the freedom of the press when, in reality, they are defending the freedom to use their own jungle standards.

'What are you going to do today?' Jeannie asked.

'Idle.'

In the morning I was mesmerised by inactivity. I just sat in the corner of the sofa, contemplating, and watching Jeannie go through her routine of making bread: the mixing of the dough, the placing of it in tins and leaving the dough to rise on the warmth of the storage heater, and afterwards the oven, and the customary cry from her: 'Don't let me forget! Forty to forty-five minutes!'

Our kitchen is the size of a galley in a small yacht. It has everything squeezed in it to make the kitchen work easily – dishwasher, calor gas stove, Magimix, Kenwood, numerous pots and pans, special kitchen knives, all the paraphernalia that a kitchen should have, except space.

Yet there was no alternative to such a kitchen. The cottage was too small for any other kind; and it was a luxury kitchen compared to what Jeannie had to endure previously. To begin with, when she came straight from knowing the luxury of the Savoy Hotel kitchens, she had to cope with a paraffin stove and paraffin oven. Then there was the Courtier stove, followed by an Esse stove, both of which offered heating and cooking facilities; and a constant memory is of Jeannie stumbling over the legs of guests warming themselves, in order to provide them with the evening meal they expected of her.

It is on such occasions that I sympathise with the feminist housewife's cry: 'Why shouldn't we be paid for the work we do?' After all, if I were to employ someone, male or female, to work on the flower farm I would pay out over £5,000 a year. There would be overtime to pay after five o'clock, double overtime at weekends, full pay during holidays. So why should a housewife work for free? Why should Jeannie? Of course, I am joking. I also work for free. We are both, like most couples, voluntary home helps. There is no one to pay us.

My special home-help role is to cope with the heavy work. Equal pay for women is an admirable concept but there are whole areas of activity where women are at a loss. During the daffodil harvest, for instance, I often find myself in the role of indispensable man. Heavy baskets of picked daffodils stand in a distant cliff meadow. Who is to carry them back to the cottage? They are far too heavy for Jeannie and any helper. I am therefore notified, and off I go to collect them.

There are other heavy tasks that only a man can do, unless the lady is an Amazon: such as digging ditches, driving the Condor, wielding the heavy-duty brush cutter. All these are too heavy for slender Jeannie. Yet I have always to be on watch that she doesn't try to do things which she shouldn't try to do. Carrying tomato boxes from the greenhouse, for instance, or carrying an over-filled basket of weeds to the compost heap. Her heaviest weight-lifting task, however, has always concerned the flower boxes. Sixty bunches of daffodils in a box provide a problem. Jeannie will pack a box, then another, and lift it upon the first. She will continue to do this until they are six boxes deep. The sixth box is like lifting a heavy suitcase on to a railway luggage rack. She insists on doing this herself while I am out in the field picking.

'Jeannie,' I said, that morning while I idled, sitting in the corner of the sofa, watching Jeannie make her twice weekly batch of bread, sometimes wholemeal, sometimes white, and always delicious, 'how are you going to idle through the day?'

She had just put the four bread tins with the risen dough in the oven.

'I'm going back to summer,' she said happily.

'What do you mean?'

'Remember all those hours we spent picking blackberries with Fred and Merlin?'

'Of course.'

There was always much competition between us and the donkeys when we picked blackberries. A big mouth would seize a clump just when I was about to pick it.

'We've still got masses in the freezer,' Jeannie went on, 'and the other day I was reading Liz Burn's recipe for seedless blackberry jam. It sounds marvellous.'

Liz Burn is a friend of ours who writes a weekly cookery page. It is a marvel to me how cookery writers conjure up recipes week after week, month after month, year after year. Jeannie collects recipes. She has a cardboard box full of recipes. She is a connoisseur of recipe writing. It happens, however, that few of these collected recipes ever come to the dining table. She finds, when the time comes to turn the recipe into reality, that it is either too complicated, or the ingredients are impossible to obtain, or she simply hasn't the time to prepare it. She therefore turns to those cookery writers who are practical, simple to understand, and offer recipes which enhance any kind of meal. Of these Liz Burn is her favourite.

'But the blackberries will take time to de-freeze,' I said.

My memory is vague as to how we managed before the freezer age. Today it ensures that we can withstand a long-term seige provided there is no long-term electricity cut. Once we were threatened with such a cut. There had been a horrendous gale, and there were broken power lines all over Cornwall. The skilled workers of the Electricity Board worked day and night to repair them, but inevitably there were some areas which had to wait and wait for the repairs to be made. Our area was one of them. I covered our two freezers with wads of newspaper, and of course never opened them for that is the most important rule when there is a cut. Twenty-four hours, thirty-six hours, forty-eight hours . . . By this time we were getting very worried. There was a small fortune of eatables in the freezers, both in the market cost of the goods, and the time cost of all our home-grown vegetables and fruit. In growing panic I set off to the headquarters of the area Electricity Board, and told them of our plight.

'Hundreds are in just the same situation,' said a stern official.

At that moment another official appeared.

'Am I not right in thinking that you live near Tater-du Lighthouse?'

'Yes,' I replied, 'and I curse it every time I hear the fog signal sounding when it isn't necessary.'

The second official looked at his colleague.

'The lighthouse circuit ought to be a priority,' he said, then turning to me, 'we'll have it restored immediately,' and then adding with a smile, 'your freezers will have to thank the lighthouse for this!'

I have felt more friendly towards Tater-du ever since.

The blackberries in the freezer were packed in polythene bags.

'It doesn't matter about them being frozen,' said Jeannie, 'that's one of the advantages of Liz's recipe.'

'What is it?'

'I'll tell you.'

And she did so. Cover the bottom of a preserving pan with about half an inch of water, put in the frozen blackberries and cook very slowly until the juice runs. Add a large apple peeled and sliced or a small carton of frozen cooked apple. Cook the fruit until very soft, drain off the juice and measure it (put the fruit through a strainer). Then to every pint of juice add one pound of sugar, put into a clean pan and bring to the boil and cook until the juice thickens. Keep a wooden spoon handy to skim off any scum. In order to judge when the jam has set, pour a little into a cold saucer. When it

106

wrinkles at the side and does not move when the saucer is tilted, the jam is done. Then pour into warm dry jars.

Summer scents accompany the process; and during my idle morning, snow thick outside, watching Jeannie, I was once again wandering Oliver land on a sunny day, bag in my hand, competing with Fred and Merlin for the juiciest blackberries.

I too am a cook. I am a cook as a result of my weakness for gadgets, useful gadgets. I have told, for instance, how my metal detector has discovered items of interest, such as our lost silver knife; and the other day it detected a screwdriver I had just bought, but which I had dropped in the grass. I have other gadgets. I have a hand-size radio which picks up the voices of airliner pilots as they pass over Minack to and from the Americas. I have a ship-to-shore radio, acquired after the Mousehole lifeboat disaster, which will monitor the voice signals of any May Day emergency at this end of the Channel, or in the Irish Sea. I have also a Citizen Band Radio which operates from the Volvo. I had this installed because of some remarkable stories I was told of its value. They concerned road accidents. A car with a CB radio can report an accident immediately, however distant the driver may be from a telephone, at whatever hour. One story described how an overturned car was found after midnight on a remote road. No telephone anywhere. But the driver who discovered the accident had CB. Help was on the way within minutes.

I have not, fortunately, experienced as yet such a fearsome accident. I did, however, one day find fifty steers running around crazily on a main road. Rather shyly, I turned to the microphone of my CB. Perhaps I should explain that all CB users have their own call sign, a 'handle' it is called in CB parlance. My 'handle', and for some reason it makes Jeannie laugh, is 'Daffodil'.

Thus, when I saw these steers careering about the road, aware that danger could at any moment result, I switched on my CB, tuned to the appropriate channel, and started hearing a strange voice, my own voice, saying into the

107

microphone: 'Daffodil calling! Daffodil calling!' Then I added the magic figures: 'Ten-thirty-four,' which meant my call was an emergency.

Within seconds I had a reply.

'This is Happy Valley, this is Happy Valley! What's the trouble?'

I told him, and he promptly informed the police; and to my amazement, within five minutes, a police car arrived and dealt with the situation.

My gadget interest has not always pleased Jeannie. I am a cook, for instance, only because I am a pressure cooker addict. Jeannie is terrified of pressure cookers, and my early experiences with them helped to justify her terror. The first model I had blew up. The second model, acquired some time later when memory of the first had faded, burnt its contents to a cinder because I had temporarily forgotten it was on the stove, and so failed to turn off the heat in time. These incidents confirmed Jeannie's conviction that a pressure cooker was the one cooking implement that should be kept well away from a kitchen.

In due course, however, my gadget mind became interested in a third model, an up-to-date model with one feature which particularly attracted me. It was a British made Prestige pressure cooker, and its special feature was an automatic timer. Thus, unlike the earlier models, a bell automatically rang when the allotted time of the cooking had been completed; and at the same time the steam inside the cooker was automatically released. I was fascinated. I was under the pressure cooker spell again; and, without telling Jeannie, I went out and bought one.

I returned to the cottage, and unpacked it; and there was horror on Jeannie's face.

'Oh no,' she cried out, 'you're not going to try that thing again!'

I then made a grave mistake. I was so excited by my purchase that I felt impelled to set it into immediate action. I ought to have waited. I ought to have perused the instructions which accompanied the pressure cooker. Instead I impatiently wanted to show it off to Jeannie, and to prove to her that a pressure cooker was the finest means of cooking, both from an economic point of view because of the time saved and in fuel used, and because of the natural flavours which resulted.

I unpacked the pressure cooker from its cardboard box, placed a three-pound gammon in it, filled the cooker partly with water, put it on the calor gas ring, then waited to show Jeannie a triumphant result.

I had made, alas, a colossal error. I had put too much water into the cooker, and I had turned on the gas far too fiercely. I had noted that the cooking time was twelve minutes per pound; and so the gammon should have been ready in thirty-six minutes. Twenty minutes had gone by when there was an explosion in the kitchen. It was as if a volcano had erupted. Steam, accompanied by a roaring, hissing sound, enveloped the kitchen end of the sitting room, and I had to fumble, blind, to switch off the gas.

'I am sorry,' I said to Jeannie, feeling foolish. 'I promise you it will be all right next time.'

I chose a morning when Jeannie had gone shopping for the next time. As soon as I saw the car disappear up the lane I set to work, knowing that I had two or three hours on my own; and so, should there be another disaster, I would have time to cover up any traces.

I had decided to make minestrone soup. I collected the pressure cooker, prepared the various ingredients, then followed the cooking method precisely. I fried a rasher of bacon gently in the base of the cooker, then cooked a chopped onion in the bacon fat until lightly brown, adding carrots, a turnip, parsley, a leek and tomatoes. All were gently cooked for five minutes. At that point I added one and a half pints of white stock I made from a chicken cube and an ounce of spaghetti; and after that I put the lid on the cooker, dialled the timer for eight minutes pressure cooking . . . and hoped for the best.

Three hours later Jeannie returned from her Penzance visit, proceeded to tell me as to how she had fared, dealt with Ambrose who always expected chopped liver on a shopping day, and then turned to me, saying: 'And what have you been doing?'

It was now lunchtime; and so I produced my minestrone soup.

She had one sip, then looked at me in astonishment.

'Derek!' she said, 'I can't believe it . . . This soup is delicious!'

My confidence has grown and grown since that day. I am now an accomplished pressure cooker cook; and this has resulted in a subtle change of evening procedure. No longer am I assured of an evening meal without having to take any part in its preparation. There will be a casual remark from Jeannie in the morning: 'I took out the topside from the freezer last night.' Topside of beef has always looked tempting but, for me, tasteless. Not any more.

'You want me to do it?'

'Of course.'

Jeannie, in fact, has become a pressure cooker convert. She admires my pioneer cooking qualities. She praises

110

without qualification the flavour of the results. But there is one aspect she remains shy of – the control of the pressure cooker itself. Thus she will happily prepare the ingredients, but as soon as they are placed in the pressure cooker she will run. It has always been part of the charm of my life with Jeannie that she can combine being brilliantly competent and sensible on the one hand, yet wayward and seductively feminine on the other.

The topside, though I do not wish to boast, plays only a minor part in my pressure cooker menu. I warm fat in the cooker, place the topside in it and cook it for a few minutes, browning it all over. I take it out, drain the fat away, put the topside back on a trivet, and pour in stock and, like the gammon, the topside is pressurised at twelve minutes per pound.

As my confidence has grown, as Jeannie's admiration has increased, the pressure cooker menu I can offer has become wider and wider. There are, however, two items of which I am particularly proud.

I am particularly proud, firstly, of my part in presenting a boiled chicken with parsley sauce. I garnish the chicken (seven minutes of pressure cooking per pound) when I put it into the cooker with celery, a shallot, carrots and any herb available; and when the cooking is completed, when the bell has rung and the steam automatically released, there is a most tender, tasty chicken. At this stage Jeannie enters the scene. She collects the liquid from the pressure cooker and makes it into a most delicious, creamy, parsley sauce. It is an epicure's dish.

The other item concerns cucumber soup, soup that was Jeannie's speciality, soup which was stored out of season in the freezer, and only served when the occasion merited it.

There was, however, a drawback about this soup; and this was the length of time it took to prepare it. On hot summer days, plants prolific with fruit, I would be daily carrying an armful to Jeannie, dropping them in front of her, jokingly saying: 'Here's some more to keep you busy!' Understandably she grew to dislike cucumber time because she found that it took, from the beginning of the preparation to the final straining of the soup, three hours for every two cucumbers.

It was now that I came to her aid with my pressure cooker. I guessed that if I could devise the right recipe I could prepare the soup in a fraction of the time; and so I experimented. I had it wrong the first time. I had one of those volcano explosions; and the contents made a mess of the kitchen. So I made modifications in the time limit, and the gas flame strength; and the result earned such applause from Jeannie that I felt like doffing my imaginary chief's hat.

My method is to peel two large cucumbers, cut them into chunks, slice also a small onion and a large potato, then gently cook them in two ounces of butter in the base of the cooker. After about three minutes pour in a pint of milk, fix the lid, and put the timer on five minutes. Also (a bit technical but not really) turn the pressure level to its slot of reducing pressure slowly. After the pressure cooker has rung its bell and released the lid, put the mushy contents through a liquidiser, and afterwards, as you pour it into a bowl, it is best to put it also through a sieve.

And the time involved? Three-quarters of an hour from peeling the first cucumber to pouring the soup into a bowl.

An idle morning was followed by an idle afternoon, an enjoyable afternoon though it was to end abruptly. I set out to browse through the bookshelves; and after a while I found myself picking out books by those who had been to Minack, those who had been greeted by us as they arrived in front of the cherry tree; and as I browsed I made remarks to Jeannie about them.

There was Howard Spring, for instance, who came down the winding lane in a breakdown van, and jumped off in front of the cherry tree waving a bottle of champagne. Marion, his wife, was with him.

'Why,' I said to Jeannie, my memory blank, 'did they arrive for lunch in a breakdown van?'

'They had gone to look at St Buryan church before

coming to us. Then the taxi broke down, so Jack Lee at the garage offered to give them a lift.'

Their method of arrival was surprising because they were a sedate couple. They lived a well-ordered life at their home, the White Cottage, in Falmouth, and I never went there without feeling I was not far from being in the Victorian era. Howard would write every day from nine till one; then lunch, followed by pottering in the large garden, one of the famous Cornish gardens which was regularly opened to the public on behalf of charities. Then at half past four, punctually, Howard would feed his cats. After a high tea Marion would then type out what Howard had written in the morning; and he would make notes for the next morning's work.

My favourites among his novels are *My Son, My Son,* which made his name as a novelist, and *These Lovers Fled Away.* He was a natural storyteller, leading you expectantly on from page to page, and creating his characters with such reality that you yourself came to believe that you were part of the story. In his time, a novelist did not tailor a novel with film or television rights in view. Nor was the method of fact-fiction resorted to, fact-fiction which confuses the uninitiated as to what is historically true or invention. Howard, like the great novelists of the past, wrote from the heart – an old-fashioned storyteller, if you like.

Marion Spring was herself a writer – *Memories and Gardens, Howard,* and the charming *Frontispiece,* a story of her childhood which, when I read it, made me think of *Cranford,* Mrs Gaskell's gentle story of Victorian manners. She was a delightfully alert person, a great gardener, with many friends who found in her and in Howard a sense of comfort that the true values, those without malice, envy or greed, were mirrored in their way of life. Unexpectedly she was a great cricket fan; and once, when she was ill in bed and Jeannie and I visited her, our arrival coincided with a tense moment in a Test Match. She was watching it on television. Quite rightly we had to stop any greeting noises until the tense moment was over.

We have mementoes of Howard and Marion on a shelf which tops a bookshelf facing the doorway into the sitting room: a small pottery, black and white striped cat which used to stand on the desk of the room where he worked. Whenever he was writing, struggling to find the words and the incidents, puffing at his pipe, he would from time to time stare at this little cat. When Marion gave it to us, she described how she and Howard saw it in a Manchester antique shop a few weeks after his first novel, *Shabby Tiger*, had been published. They thought it was an omen for their future.

And there is another memento on the same shelf. When *A Drake at the Door* was first published, they gave me a beautiful Royal Doulton china model of a drake. And there are two Royal Doulton cats given to us by Michael, their son, after Marion died.

There were books by Beverley Nichols alongside those of the Springs. Marion was a great admirer of Beverley, and was anxious to meet him; and when she heard that he was visiting us one cold January, she asked us to bring him over to the White Cottage. Marion's special pride was a dolls' house, an exact replica of the White Cottage; the furnishings in exact proportion; even the miniature knives and forks were of silver. After tea Marion took Beverley to see it, and after expressing his admiration, he made a remark which only a besotted cat lover could be expected to make; a remark which in my anti-cat times, I would have considered very foolish.

On the steps outside the front door of the dolls' house was curled the miniature figure of a black cat.

'We call him Perkins,' said Marion, 'after my old black cat who is over twenty.'

Beverley paused, then stooped, picked up the tiny figure, and placed it inside the dolls' house.

'Too cold outside, Perkins,' he said, 'you're old, you must keep warm.'

There are many books by A. P. Herbert on the bookshelf. Such wit in his books, the chuckling kind of wit, no guffaw. He used to come and stay with us in August, and sit on the white seat in front of the cherry tree, and write. Here he wrote most of the musical play *The Water Gypsies*, adapted from his novel of the same title, doing so at the suggestion of Jeannie when one morning at breakfast he complained: 'I don't know what to write. Help me!' The play, with exquisite music by Vivian Ellis, would have been just as successful as their earlier hit *Bless the Bride*, except for an unexpected incident. One of the leading ladies announced she was pregnant; and the backer of the musical decided that without her, receipts would drop. He therefore withdrew the show. A little later the leading lady announced it was a false alarm. Some people are haunted all their lives by a failure for which they were in no way responsible. It is an old story. No success is achieved without luck being on your side. No success without someone who, at the exact moment, with the intuition, the promotional skill and the flair, comes into your life.

APH (and I use his initials because everyone in his famous *Punch* days used to refer to him in this way) kept urging me to write the book which was to be the first of the Minack Chronicles, *A Gull on the Roof*. He was on a visit when I said to him there was no chair in the hut where I was trying to write. I sat on a large box.

Thereupon he went into Penzance with Jeannie and bought a chair. The hut was at the bottom of the cliff meadows, close to the sea, a hut we normally used for the storing of potato seed before planting. Later that day I was sitting there when I heard coming nearer and nearer, boisterous male voices singing 'This is my lovely day' from APH's *Bless the Bride*.

The two voices soon came round the corner. One voice was that of APH. The other was that of our then Member of Parliament, Greville Howard. Between them they carried the chair, and proceeded to place it in the hut beside me.

'No excuse for more delay,' said APH. 'Now get on with it!'

It was growing dark. Jeannie was in the kitchen making a cake, and I was at the other end of the room, looking at the bookshelf behind my desk.

I picked up Mary Stewart's *The Crystal Cave*, and I remembered a summer's day when we sat with her and her husband on the bridge, listening to stories about her cat Troy; and how, because her husband was called Fred, he insisted he should have a photograph with our Fred.

Alongside *The Crystal Cave* was a copy of *All My Burning Bridges*, the wistful autobiography of Pat Phoenix. We had looked out of the window one January morning to see two strangers standing by a car in front of the cherry tree. It was the heyday of Elsie Tanner in *Coronation Street*, but as Jeannie and I never watched it on television, we did not recognise the two strangers as Pat Phoenix and her screen and real-life husband Alan Browning. They stayed for lunch, stayed all the afternoon. The beginning of a friendship with Pat.

I had put out my hand to take out another book, John Stewart Collis's *Follow the Plough*, when there was a call from the kitchen.

'Derek! There's no water coming from the tap!'

My idle afternoon had come to its abrupt end.

The pipes had frozen.

NINE

The thaw came as quickly as the snow had come. At breakfast time next morning the snow was ankle deep outside
the porch door, at tea time it had disappeared, while the lane
itself, which had given us our illusion of isolation, was
swiftly becoming a lane of mushy puddles.

'Perhaps,' I said to Jeannie hopefully, 'it will freeze again
tonight, then our isolation will return.'

It did not return.

Jeannie and I had to face reality.

Reality meant the coming of the daffodil season.

'Let's make a list of the things we'll need,' said Jeannie.

It was after supper, and we were sitting in front of the
fire. Ambrose was curled on the sofa beside me. Cherry was
in her hideout at the far end of the sitting room in the corner
behind my desk.

I picked up a pen and a notepad.

'Boxes, for a start,' I said.

Boxes, twenty-four inches long, fifteen inches wide, six
inches deep, made of strong cardboard and costing 85p
each; it is a pity that they can only be used once. There was
a time, however, when such boxes were returned to the
growers, and so they were used again and again. Freight
costs were a minor problem in those days.

117

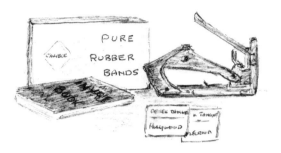

We need rubber bands,' said Jeannie, 'the normal ones, and also the small ones for the Obs.'

Obs are miniature King Alfred daffodils.

'And I'm afraid,' Jeannie went on, 'that we'll have to have another supply of metal strips. We didn't get any last year and there are only a few left.'

Many growers do without metal strips. They crowd the daffodil bunches so tight in a box that they are wedged there as if in a block. Jeannie's packing attitude is different. She believes by packing fewer bunches in a box (sixty is the number she normally aims to do), the daffodils travel better and the presentation is better. Hence, in order to keep the bunches firm in the box, she has to use a metal strip. The strip is placed across the daffodil stems, then each sharp end is pressed into the side of the box; and the end turned flush against the cardboard. Vital for her to remember to turn it flush, otherwise it is easy for anyone handling the box to cut himself.

'I need string,' I said, and put that down too on the list. I am in charge of tying the boxes, and I use a lot of string. 'And what's the label situation like?' I asked.

The labels are our hallmark. They are the size of a postcard with my name and the address stamped on it; and underneath this we write the daffodil variety, and the number of bunches. This label is stapled on one side of the box; on the other is another label with the name of the wholesaler to whom we are sending the consignment; and this wholesaler is normally J. & E. Page of Covent Garden.

'We're short of Page's,' said Jeannie, 'you had better write straight away for more. But we have plenty of our own.'

There were other items we had to check. We had to see we had a supply of staples, and that both type of staple machines were in good order. One staple machine was for stapling cards. The other kind was for stapling together each box, and this was my job because Jeannie's wrist was not strong enough. Each box was delivered in a flat state, and I then proceeded to manoeuvre the cut out design into a bottom and a top, stapling the sides together. Even my own wrist became tired after stapling twenty or thirty boxes.

We needed none of these things for a week. The daffodils were still backward, and although the snow soon cleared from the meadows and the weather became warm with a haze over the sea, we were only able to pick a bunch or two for ourselves.

Yet it is on such occasions that a sense of tranquillity combines with the excitement of anticipation; and it is a halcyon period of the year. A period of the year which hails the opportunity for individuals to recognise the beauty and the freedom on their doorstep, making one realise that the secret of human happiness lies within the individual himself, rather than in the pursuit of mass togetherness. Mass togetherness creates mass hysteria. Mass togetherness with all its razzmatazz diverts those taking part from delving into their true selves. Instead of individuals they become zombies. Slogans and banners and violence are the children of mass togetherness; and it steals from the individual the freedom to be himself.

There was, however, no tranquillity when Ambrose and Cherry faced each other, no softening in Ambrose's attitude towards her. We had to be constantly on guard, indulging in nerve-wracking efforts to keep them apart. At night we would sometimes hear terrible screams outside, and I would rush out with a torch calling out: 'Stop it, Ambrose. Stop it!' Then later I would ponder how unfair it was of me to treat Ambrose as if he was the villain. After all, Minack was his home. How would I have felt if a stranger had dumped himself in the cottage?

It was during this period that there occurred a particularly scaring incident. Jeannie and I and Ambrose had gone for a walk up the lane, then into the clover field, and on to the Ambrose Rock, upon which Ambrose jumped, topping it up with purrs. On our return I saw, as we came close to Monty's Leap, the little black figure of Cherry waiting there on the other side of the stream. Ambrose saw her too, and before we could grab him, he had sped with the speed of a greyhound after her.

Again the cry, a useless cry: 'Stop it, Ambrose!'

Cherry saw him when he was barely five yards away, and made a tactical error. Instead of darting into the under-growth on either side of the lane, she chose to test her own speed against Ambrose's speed; and so she turned and began racing up the lane towards the cottage. We watched helplessly as Ambrose gradually gained on her. True, we continued to shout; true, we both ran after them, but these were pointless gestures. Past the hydrangea bush on the left, past the door into my office; and Ambrose growing closer and closer. Poor Cherry looking so small.

Then she made a brilliant move.

Instead of continuing up the path to the cottage, she swerved to the left, and leapt on to the bottom branch of the cherry tree, then up, up to the top where she wavered in the fork of thin branches, looking down in safety on Ambrose whom many people have called the King of Minack. The King accepted the situation. The race up the lane had soothed him. It had disposed of the adrenalin which prompted it. He glanced up at the top of the tree, then wandered off, nonchalantly, giving the impression that he did not harbour a fundamental hatred for Cherry. It was just that he wanted to preserve his relationship with Jeannie and me; and, understandably, he felt it was threatened.

Humans, time and again, experience the same fears.

Couples, married or living together, experience the moment when another person enters their lives, and poses a threat. Sometimes, of course, the threat is unnoticed by the other person, so that the affair takes place without rancour, only a sense of guilt occasionally surfacing. Yet a casual affair, if denied, can easily turn into a serious one out of pique, out of frustration. A casual affair need not be a threat. Boredom with each other is the main threat in a companionship or a marriage.

Ambrose never spent much time indoors during the day. He might linger on the bed for a while after we had got up, but it was the hay in the Orlyt which was his day quarters. Thus Cherry had the world of the cottage to herself for the most part of the day, and she relished it; and she grew in confidence.

She was still not a cuddly cat. She still was stand-offish when Jeannie or I wanted to treat her with special affection. No sitting on a lap. No picking up and hugging. Yet her confidence was growing . . .

For instance, when Ambrose made a day appearance in the cottage, and this might be at lunchtime or at teatime when he was expecting some item from his regular menu, Cherry, sitting on the arm of a chair, would spit at him.

Her manners upset Jeannie and myself, and we would tell her how we felt . . . But Ambrose, and this was the charm of him, ignored the insults. Angry though he might be when she confronted him outside, he seemed willing to accept her indoors. It was strange. Fireworks outdoors, tolerance within.

Her spitting at him, I guess, was due to fear, a case of attack being the best form of defence, but it was a risky attitude for her to adopt. It was even riskier when one morning I saw her slap him with a paw as he passed her. It was breakfast time. Ambrose, once a fish-only cat, had developed a taste for Best Ever Whiskas; and Jeannie had opened a tin, spooned out part of it for Ambrose, part of it for Cherry, placing one saucer by the kitchen for Ambrose, the other in the porch for Cherry.

Each had their fill, then Ambrose, licking his lips in satisfaction, walked into the porch, expecting one of us to open the door so that he could go off to his daytime quarters.

As he passed Cherry, out came the paw. He was astonished. It touched him just below the ear, and I watched with amazement his reaction. No question of retaliation. He just gave her a filthy look. I opened the door and he stalked out.

Cherry's games were the usual kitten games. She chased her tail, chased her shadow, liked tossing a left-over holly leaf up in the air, and would leap at a chair and start climbing up it as if she was a cat mountaineer. 'Stop it, Cherry,' Jeannie would cry out, 'that's our last good cover, and you're ruining it!'

This particular incident raised the question as to her C Level progress. She had so far done well. No bird had been caught, no live mouse brought into the cottage; and she had so far only displayed one weakness. Like Ambrose she was a rotovator of the carpet. Little plots of churned up carpet had steadily increased since her arrival. Nothing could be done about it. We just had to accept that we had a couple of gardeners living in the cottage.

Cherry also created a game of her own which at first startled Knocker the gull. If the casement window in the porch was ajar she would take on the role of an acrobat, leaping up the open end of the window, squeezing through the gap at the top, then on to the glass roof of the porch. All this was done with a great deal of noise and a great deal of shuddering of the casement window. The performance was not that of cat-like grace, far too much strain and effort for that; and I certainly did not like her doing it. Nor did I like her next move.

This was to jump on to the roof itself, then wander about it with the same sort of ease as if she was wandering on the ground. It is possible, of course, that she thought that the roof, being free of Ambrose danger, was a pleasant place to be. She had not, however, in those first days realised that

Knocker, in the same way as Ambrose on the ground, considered the roof his special preserve.

A similar unawareness had occurred some years before with an unhappy result. A predecessor of Knocker had a somewhat savage nature, and indeed Monty, who was with us at the time, was terrified of him. In the spring he was particularly vicious, and he would swoop down low over Monty as he scurried along the path. Monty, however, came to no harm. It was a male chaffinch which was the victim. The chaffinch was at the far end of the apex of the roof, chirping cheerfully, when the gull, irritated perhaps by the noise, began to walk along the apex towards it. Why the chaffinch did not take notice of the danger has always puzzled me. Maybe it was mesmerised into inaction, like a rabbit in the glare of headlights. In any case it did not move. The gull came nearer and nearer, then thrust out its beak and gobbled it.

Cherry, however, had a gull of a different nature to face. Knocker's one fault was his knocking; and he had now been knocking on the porch glass roof for so long that it is surprising a pane has not crashed to the floor. As it is there is a crack or two, and no wonder. When he hits the glass with his beak, it sounds as if a hammer is being used. Yet there was no harm in this. It was just a way of calling attention to himself, a way of demanding slices of bread, any kind of left-overs, in fact.

It was a left-over fish skin which was the cause of Knocker's meeting with Cherry. Cherry had performed her acrobatic act up the casement window at a moment when Knocker was squatting on the chimney; and Jeannie had just thrown up the fish skin.

Cats, however well fed, are always at the ready to be scavengers. I have been appalled by the behaviour of un-named Minack cats whom I have found devouring left-overs which they had no justification to devour.

It was so on this occasion. Cherry was there on the sloping roof, saw the fish skin, and advanced . . . choosing the exact moment when Knocker had decided to descend from the square chimney top to collect it himself. There was no doubt as to the winner. Cherry had one glance at Knocker, and made a roof-running exit.

Knocker, recently, got into trouble with another left-over object. Perhaps, however, I am wrong. Perhaps it wasn't Knocker. It could have been Philip. The trouble is that as soon as a normal routine is changed, one has difficulty in identifying the gulls concerned.

In this case, Jeannie had taken the usual kitchen debris down to the dustbin but had paused for a moment at what we now call the cats' kitchen, placing the debris outside while she stepped inside to collect a plate of fish for Ambrose. In the few seconds she was inside, one of the gulls had swept down from the roof, and dived his beak into the debris.

A part of this debris was the string netting which covers gammon when you buy it. The custom is to cook the gammon, still enclosed in the string netting, then discard the netting when the gammon is cooked.

That is what Jeannie had done. She had not, however, bargained for a gull to descend so suddenly to where she had momentarily left the debris – and seize the netting.

It happened to be me who saw the result. I looked up at the roof, and saw this gull with its beak emmeshed in the string netting. It couldn't move its beak. It was going to suffocate.

Then came a miracle moment. The helpless gull was joined by another gull; and this gull proceeded to peck at the string netting until it suddenly became free and dropped to the ground.

Jeannie and I were watching. It was one of those experiences which draw you away from surface standards, a realisation that not only humans have the will to save others.

We watched the string netting drop to the ground, then, just as we were moving forward to pick it up, the gull, the gull which had been at risk, swooped down on the netting which had nearly killed him, and swallowed it. Foolish gull.

On 7 February we sent away our first box of daffodils, a box of Magnificence, a fortnight later than the previous year. We picked them from a meadow which regularly produces our first daffodils, the bottom meadow of a series of descending meadows in what we call the Merlin cliff.

It was called the Merlin cliff because when Mingoose Merlin first came to Minack we took him and Fred for a walk along the coastal path towards our western boundary, an uncultivated field known from time immemorial as the 'onion meadow'. Just before reaching the meadow there is a gap which leads to the path, and then on down the cliff at the side of the descending meadows. Merlin, on that first walk, saw the gap, dashed through it, followed by Fred. They raced down the path, and up again. At that moment the *Scillonian* was passing by on her way to the islands. Merlin was fascinated. He stood staring, quite still, at the first ship he had seen in his life. From then on we referred to these meadows as the Merlin cliff.

We were on our own for the first two weeks. We could cope with the early daffodils without outside help; and we would be off to the meadows when the sun was rising over the Lizard, and the Lizard light was blinking, behaving as if it was still night time. We would each take a meadow, then bent double we would start to pick, missing out stems in the row which were too short. There was no fear at this stage of the season that the buds would be too plump, too close to opening into bloom; and so the stems we picked had buds as thin as pencils. Jeannie hated to pick them in this condition, but as I was commercially minded I knew this had to be done. The flower markets of today insist on buds, and such bunches of buds do have the advantage of lasting longer. But a word of warning. In the early part of the year, over Christmas time also, the markets are flooded with daffodils forced in hangar-like greenhouses. They may be called daffodils, but they look like grass. They sometimes never bloom, just die as a bud.

I am, of course, prejudiced against such forcing methods because they take away the romance of daffodils. In my London days, the sight of the first daffodils in the shops and the flower stalls soothed me; and my imagination conjured up the picture of the daffodil meadows in the Scilly Islands and Cornwall, and the picture was an antidote to the hectic, superficial way of life that I led. Daffodils then came from a natural scene. That was the source of their inspiration.

I wonder what I would have said had I foreseen that one day I myself would be working at such a source, bent double, picking with my left hand, transferring the stems to my right hand when there were too many to hold; and to have someone of the sophistication of Jeannie (Danny Kaye wrote the foreword of her *Meet Me at the Savoy*) also bent double in a neighbouring meadow; and before breakfast.

'How are you doing?' I called out.

'Better than I expected. My basket is half full.'

Then a pause as we continued our task.

'I've got some gaps here,' I called out again.

Gaps are caused by the dying out of the bulbs, either by the evil bulb fly, or simply by the lack of moisture in the cliff soil during the summer or, more rarely, by bulb eelworm. In the case of dying-out patches in our meadows, they seemed to be due to hot, very dry conditions in the summer. Thus, when there is a wet summer, unlike the holiday-makers, we have a compensation.

There would be long silences as we picked. Our action was automatic so that as we moved along the rows, our minds roamed in the uncontrollable way of dreams. I would find myself, for instance, without any logical reason picking a stem, and suddenly associating it with a girl I had known, years, years ago. Or there were other times when I picked a stem, or more accurately was about to pick a stem, that a face appeared in my mind which angered me – a face which, real or imagined, represented a person who had cheated us. Such a stem, as a consequence of my uncontrollable roaming mind, was picked unfairly with a snap.

There was a timelessness about our task, all flower seasons merged into one season; and around us were the sights and scents which were like old friends. There was a high rock of blue elvin at one end of the meadows where we were picking; and at the bottom of it there was a tunnel through brambles used by foxes on their travels along the cliff. As always there was the scent of a fox when I picked close to it. A few yards away, below the rock, there was a cluster of Scilly Whites, the bulbs thrown there no doubt in the war time when potatoes took precedence in the meadows. I looked at the cluster and noted, as in years before, the buds would soon perfume the base of the rock of blue elvin. There were other friends to note. As I went up a path between the beds I found the patch of wild violets which I always knew would be there; and in the bank at the bottom of the meadow spreadeagled in the grass were the leaves of primroses, a single bloom of yellow in their centre.

Behind me as I picked was the murmuring sea; and the fishing boats, after a night's fishing, hurrying back to catch the market at Newlyn. Gulls floated in the sky. Gannets, in threes and fours, pounded their wings majestically west-wards.

'My basket is full,' called Jeannie, 'have you any room in yours?'

'You're much quicker than me. I'm only half full.'

Below us were the rocks, and the pool we swim in; and where, when we first came to Minack, Jeannie, a celebrity because much had been written about her life at the Savoy, used to rehearse a speech she was due to make when opening the Mousehole Sports Regatta. She would call out her speech as she swam in the pool, and she would call out the speech again, standing on a rock, with the sea as an audience. Jeannie has never liked to make speeches, has never wished to thrust herself forward, always preferring to rely upon her feminity to gain her conquests. Charles B. Cochran, Noël Coward's favourite showman, pressed her to become one of his prestigious 'Young Ladies', equivalent of the Gaiety Girls, but Jeannie was not interested. She would have enhanced the group of very pretty, slim Young Ladies if Cochran had seen her standing naked on a rock, rehearsing a speech for the opening of the Mousehole Sports Regatta.

In those early days there was more time for us to dis-appear from the environment of the cottage, and seep up the sun down on the rocks; and plunge into the pool, and dry ourselves in the sea air without towels; or wander across the rocks, exploring. There was no threat of a British Air-ways helicopter passing overhead in those times, or of a silent-engined diver's craft suddenly taking up station close off shore. Boats made engine noises in those times. There was time to hide when a passing boat was heard.

On one of those wanderings across the rocks, we made an extraordinary discovery. It was not many yards away from the pool in which we swam – chiselled a half-inch deep in a sea-worn rock of granite that formed part of a small ravine which ate into the cliff, were the initials J.N.

Jeannie's maiden name is Jean Nicol.

The weather was not always calm when we picked

daffodils down the Merlin cliff. We have picked in southerly gales which made us unsteady as we bent double. We have picked on early mornings when it was so cold that we wore mittens, and still had to pause now and then to blow hot breath on our fingers. Sometimes, too, there has been a thick fog, and then the Tater-du fog signal bellows in our ears every twenty seconds; and sometimes we have had to pick while torrents of rain have penetrated our anoracks. Always, whatever the weather, when our baskets are full, I have to take the long trudge up the cliff, then along the path to the cottage, a full basket in either hand, Jeannie behind me.

'I'll watch out,' she will say, 'for any stems which may drop out.'

Yet, at the end of the day, it is the sense of reality that always gives us immeasurable pleasure. Each daffodil in the basket is on its way to give happiness in some room of a city; and there is this great satisfaction in providing a happiness which comes from the earth. There is no fake about it, no artificiality. It is true.

If I was a rational person, however, I would find fault in my remarks. Society is geared to make profits for its survival rather than to strive to improve the emotional quality of life. Picking daffodils in cliff meadows may help to improve such quality, but the financial returns do not warrant the expense of doing so. On our own we make a profit, but as soon as the field daffodils are ready for picking, and we have to engage help, the case for picking these daffodils becomes, each year, less and less justified. It may be better to leave them unpicked.

There are two reasons for this. One is over-production of daffodils. The large growers with their factory-type growing methods are principally concerned in selling bulbs. Selling of the flowers is a bonus, but it is a bonus which swamps the market, bringing down the prices for the rest of us. The other reason is in the increasing forced cost of labour. Picking and bunching cannot be mechanised; and however quick a picker and buncher may be there is a limit to the number of bunches that can be handled in an hour. Hence there is an inevitable meeting point between the labour cost per box and the market price obtained per box; and when this happens there is no sense in picking the daffodils.

One wonders, when faced with such miniature employment problems, whether those who endlessly talk about solving unemployment are really aware what causes it. There are thousands of people like myself who will never again employ a regular worker because of the official regulations regarding their rights; and because of the wage, whether the business is having a successful time or not, which the employer is enforced to pay.

There is also the myth among many political and union circles that everyone who is unemployed is a paragon of virtue – eager, willing to learn, punctual, prepared to give value for the wage. There are many employers who have found that this just does not come to pass. They may see a candidate for a job, accept him, name the day of starting work; and he doesn't turn up. Or there are others who have found that their new employee is sulky, disruptive, and lazy.

My own simplistic view is that more encouragement should be given to those on the unemployment list who are willing to adopt the self-employment attitude. Such people accept terms of employment which suit themselves and any employer; and there are no union *voyeurs* to upset the relationship.

We were fortunate in those who worked for us during the daffodil season. Margaret, the potter who lives at the end of our lane and who, before she married her London taxi driver husband George, now known as one of the best potters in Cornwall, was trained as a dressmaker at the famous establishment in Bond Street, The White House. Margaret, always enthusiastic, always wanting to pick as many daffodils as possible whatever the weather conditions, had also the function of looking after Fred and Merlin if we went away; and looking after Ambrose.

130

Then there was Joan, equally enthusiastic, the one-time London secretary who used to read the Minack Chronicles as she ate her sandwiches on a bench in Lincoln's Inn Fields. Joan shared with Margaret the task of looking after Fred, Merlin and Ambrose; and she was now about to have a task of special responsibility.

Once a year Jeannie and I usually shed our country egos, and adopt London ones. It is a business occasion and, thanks to Jeannie, we stay at the Savoy Hotel Company's prestigious hotel, Claridge's. We always set off from Minack reluctantly, shedding our country egos when we halt in Hyde Park after passing through Queen's Gate, where we get out of the car, stretch, Jeannie looks in the mirror, and I put on my town suit jacket. When we feel becalmed after the six-hour journey, we set off on the remaining short distance to Claridge's. From then on we live in luxury, and in the company of staff who are our friends. Our main task, however, is to make contact with those who could increase our income.

There were, understandably, complications surrounding this year's London visit. On other occasions, though concern existed, there was cat harmony at Minack. On this occasion we were going to leave Ambrose and Cherry alone together. This was not a harmonious situation. They may have hinted at better relations developing, but hardly enough to justify their being left on their own. Hence Joan agreed that after Margaret had arrived in the morning and had attended to Fred and Merlin, she would come soon after, and stay as long as she could, as a caretaker for Ambrose and Cherry. But there were still the nights. How were Ambrose and Cherry going to react when they found themselves on their own at night?

Jeannie and I had to shut our minds to that question. We would be away for only three days. In those three days we might be able to make contacts which would ensure endless supplies of Best Ever Whiskas for them both; and we had also been invited to the 'Authors of the Year' party annually given by Hatchards of Piccadilly, the most renowned booksellers in the world. For me this was to be a special occasion. The first time I was invited to the Hatchard's party was after *A Donkey in the Meadow* had been published; and on the jacket was a very young Fred. This time the book was *A Quiet Year*, and on the jacket was an older Fred, Merlin beside him, looking over a bank of daffodils near the cottage. A bridge of time.

We planned to leave at six-thirty on a Tuesday morning, the last of the daffodils having been sent away the previous week. On Monday evening the suitcases were packed, and we went to bed early. Neither Ambrose nor Cherry were indoors. We had looked for them, called them, but they obviously had other matters on their minds, and they did not respond to us.

'They'll come in before long,' Jeannie said confidently.

I did not go to sleep immediately. I lay awake, thinking of the hassle of the next three days, of the efforts Jeannie and I would be making to try to impress people of influence, people who live under such business pressure that they only have time to make superficial judgements. Our long-ago London lives would be repeated. We would be going through the motions of living. It would not be real.

My mind was thus roaming when there was a prolonged scream outside, like the sound of tearing calico.

'Jeannie,' I called, struggling out of bed, 'the cats are at it again!'

She too had been lying awake.

'I can't go, I can't go tomorrow!'

I was shaken by her vehemence.

'We have to go . . . We can't get out of it now.'

The scream had died away, and there was silence.

'What will happen tomorrow night, and the next night, and the night after?'

'Keep calm,' I said, 'I'll go out and see what's happening.'

I went outside with a torch, saw a serene Ambrose, and he followed me back indoors. A half an hour later I got up again, and went into the spare bedroom. Cherry was curled on the bed. She had returned through her bathroom entrance.

'All's well,' I reported to Jeannie; and went to sleep.

At half past six the next morning, the suitcases were in the car, and we were ready to go, when I saw the surprising figure of Joan coming down the lane.

'I forgot to ask,' she explained anxiously, 'what temperature does Ambrose have his milk?'

We deposited our London egos at Claridge's in suite number 416/417, overlooking the corner of Davies Street and Brook Street; and as soon as we had settled in – luggage unpacked, drinks brought in by Kurt the floor waiter, glass in hand as we sat in comfortable chairs – my London ego had a setback.

'I don't want to move from here,' I said to Jeannie. 'I want to remain cocooned in these rooms just as if we were at home.'

'You really are silly. You come all this way and start losing your nerve. We've a job to do, see lots of people, try to influence them in our favour, and if we make a success of it we'll be able to remain cocooned at Minack.'

Jeannie was over by a corner table looking at a card attached to a vase in which blue and yellow irises were mingled with pink carnations.

'They're from Michael,' she said.

Michael Bentley, celebrated manager of Claridge's, was a long-time friend.

At this moment there was a knock at the door, and a girl appeared with another vase of flowers, this time of tulips, and they were the gift of our publishers, Michael Joseph.

'What a welcome we're having!' said Jeannie, then turning to me, 'Now get rid of all that cocooning!'

Claridge's is not one of those city-based hotels which reflect the bustle of an air terminal. Claridge's is discrete. It is not a functional hotel catering for those who travel in haste. It imbues an atmosphere of elegance, an old-fashioned elegance in the minds of some who are not accustomed to the kind of personal service it provides. There is a log-fire in the foyer in the winter, there are glorious arrangements of flowers at all times; and I remember once when we were there that I passed by an old man polishing a walnut chest which stood against the wall in the corridor opposite the lift.

'That's a fine chest,' I said.

'Yes,' he replied, as he went on polishing, 'I've been looking after this chest for thirty years.'

Our suite had a sitting room as large as the floor space of the cottage. You came into it through a hallway, and there was a door from the hallway into the bedroom, as large as the sitting room; and another door led into the bathroom. On the walls of the sitting room were prints of London in early times; and there was a marble mantlepiece on which ticked an early nineteenth-century French clock. The thick carpet was of myrtle green, and the curtains were of an exquisite heavy damask material, a design of primrose yellow, apricot and green. All the furniture was antique; and dominating the sitting room was the marble fireplace where, in a winter mood, you could have a log fire.

The telephone buzzed and Jeannie picked up the receiver – a message from a business contact saying he would be calling on us at half past five.

'Darling,' said Jeannie, knowing that such a visit could be important, 'that's marvellous news. We'll keep the first part of the evening free for him.'

I looked across to her standing there, seemingly as young and eager as when I first knew her in Room 205 of the Savoy Hotel running the public relations of the Savoy, Claridge's and the Berkeley; and I said to myself that had it not been for Jeannie I would not now be sitting in a Claridge's suite. Then my mind went back to that evening when I first saw her.

She was sitting at a table in the River Room of the Savoy, windows boarded up because it was Blitz time and an air raid was in progress. Carroll Gibbons and his band were playing 'These Foolish Things'; and Jeannie was at a table a dozen yards from me, a Naval officer and a Wren as her companions. She seemed to be staring at me, and if it was not at me, it was someone very near me. I was in uniform, and had my MI5 secretary as my companion; and I became so intrigued by this slim, colleen-like girl paying me such attention that I left my secretary at the table, making the excuse that as I knew the Wren slightly I wanted to have a word with her. The Wren obligingly introduced me to the colleen-like girl; and thus, in such a way, an everlasting love affair began. However, my approach to her was not very romantic. On being told that she was the Savoy PRO, I blurted out: 'I've just had a book published called *Time Was Mine*. Can you arrange for it to be on the bookstall?'

My own first visit to Claridge's was a result of my being a Deb's Delight. My rooms in London were at 38 Cranley Gardens in South Kensington; and I arrived there at the age of nineteen after I had become a clerk in Unilever. I knew no one in London except one family who had a daughter who was about to be launched into the frivolous turmoil of a debutante season. Snobbishness dominated such seasons, a desperate anxiety also on the part of mothers that their daughters met young men whom they considered to possess the proper background. It was a period when opportunist young men could be assured of free evenings from April to early July. It was fortunate that I was considered to have the proper background, for I needed the free evenings of entertainment, the free food. My pay was thirty shillings a week. Thus I was grateful to the girl and her mother who introduced me into being a Deb's Delight. There was a kind of chain-letter response. I was invited to more and more parties. Mothers considered me safe. They could rely on me to be respectful towards their daughters. Their reason? I had been educated at Harrow.

Claridge's, however, remained a gilded, unapproachable sanctum until one day I was invited by a rich family to the dinner before their daughter's dance; and I arrived wearing my white tie and tails by bus. In these tails were deep pockets, and these pockets were to be very useful later on when I left Unilever and was out of work. I was still, at the time, a Deb's Delight; and as dawn broke over the debutante's dance I was attending, I would fill these pockets from the buffet table, thus ensuring I had food for the following day. On one occasion, however, I was found out. I was asked by my hostess to be her partner for the last dance; and as we waltzed round, the contents of the deep pockets in my tails spattered the dance floor.

I arrived at Claridge's, walked nervously up the entrance steps to the foyer, and was then ushered into a private room where there were gathered a number of faces whom I recognised from reading society magazines. This, I realised, was a very special occasion; and when I discovered that the daughter, the belle of the ball, had chosen me as her special guest, placing me at the dinner table on her right, I was filled with apprehension. Her parents, as a result of my Harrow credentials, had obviously passed me as being a reliable partner for their daughter. I had, however, on entering the private room, recognised another guest, a lady who had been present when I had an unfortunate experience a few weeks before. It had occurred, as it happened, in a Davies Street flat only a few yards from Claridge's. I had been to a cocktail party, then went on to a dinner party at the flat.

I fell asleep over the soup.

Jeannie and I now sat spruced, awaiting the arrival of our business contact at half past five. Assorted salted almonds, little cheese biscuits, a carafe of white wine, a bottle of whisky, and so on, were on a table ready for our guest to choose from.

'Jeannie,' I said, 'I wonder if he has done his homework.'

It is always awkward when one meets someone who is of potential importance, yet who knows little about one's life. Then, as a form of nervous reaction, one finds oneself gushing out facts, without doing justice to the nuances which fill one's life.

A person who did not fail us in this respect was Roy Plomley. When we met for lunch, before going to the BBC to record my interview with him as a castaway on Desert Island Discs, I found he had meticulously done his homework; and as a result I felt at ease with him. His ability to be kind and sensitive, and interested in his castaway, was the reason for his prolonged success. His approach was never superficial. He never skimmed the surface of a subject. A special aspect of his approach was contained in the letters he wrote beforehand to the Castaway. They were written in his own handwriting and, when I received my own first letter from him, I instinctively felt I was about to make a new friend. It was a very happy moment for me when I learnt he had included me in his book *Plomley's Pick*, forty of his favourite castaways.

It was now twenty past five. Jeannie and I had a pleasant feeling of anticipation. Our new business contact, we thought, was about to arrive; and at that moment the telephone buzzed. I picked up the receiver.

'Yes ... Yes ... You're held up? You can't make it? Not even later? What a shame!'

I turned round to Jeannie.

'Damn,' I said crossly.

But she was laughing.

'You'll have to put up with me on my own this evening!'

On that first evening, the prospect of a four-day visit seemed to stretch endlessly before us; and yet, in retrospect, when the time came to pack and go home, it seemed like a period of five minutes. Then, as we drove home, we held an inquest on our impressions.

Fear dominated my own impression. Fear of burglary, fear in the streets. Strange to think there was a time when one was able to roam the streets in a careless mood at night; and yet, on this visit, we were advised it would be unwise to walk the streets of Mayfair after dark.

This change from casual happiness to fear, after a world war in which many of my friends were ready to die for freedom, is the fundamental change in my lifetime; that, and the emergence of the multi-racial society. Other scenes are basically the same except they are more hectically pursued. There was always a rat race, always ambitious people ready to doublecross each other, always those who revelled in the adrenalin of wheeler dealing, always those who were insensitive when dealing with others, always those who were snobs, socially or intellectually, always those who dashed from promotion party to promotion party.

'The glamour and hospitality,' I wrote when Jeannie and I left London for Minack, 'act as a narcotic, doping the finer instincts of living, and in the grey hours of early morning you lie awake painfully aware that you live in a flashy world where truth and integrity are for the most part despised, where slickness reigns supreme.'*

There were two incidents during our visit which I will specially remember, and one of them concerned the time

* From *A Gull on the Roof.*

139

when I was a member of MI5. I knew in the early days of the war a girl called Joan Miller who was in her early twenties, very pretty with widely set apart eyes and a still manner. I was no intimate friend of hers, but she worked in a secret section of MI5 with a base in a Dolphin Square flat, where I also worked from a flat. Her chief was the mysterious Captain Maxwell Knight who ran a number of undercover agents and who numbered each agent with the prefix M (Ian Fleming was a friend of his and Bond was partly modelled on Max).

I had a great admiration for Max. In Joan Miller's case she was hypnotised by him. Max had a remarkable gift of reaching into the depths of a person's character without ever having met the person concerned. I used to have long conversations with him concerning some individual he suspected of being a potential enemy agent, and he would have such knowledge of the man or woman that one would have thought they must be bosom friends.

This gift, however, was of no benefit to him in regard to Anthony Blunt. One of Max's undercover agents was Tom Driberg, William Hickey at the time, then later a Labour Member of Parliament and a peer. Driberg was known to Max as M8. Anthony Blunt happened to see a report by M8, and judged by its contents that the author was Tom Driberg. He notified his Soviet Controller, who in turn warned the British Communist Party of which Tom Driberg was pretending to be an ardent supporter. Tom Driberg was thereupon sacked from the Party; and so M8 was lost to Max. From then on Max knew there was a spy in MI5 but he was never able to trace him until, years later, Blunt made his confession.

Joan Miller had written to me before we came to London, saying she wanted to talk with me about Max, who had now died; and we made a date to meet at Claridge's. I had not seen her since those long-ago days when she was twenty-two, but she thought I could be helpful because I had known Max so well; she was writing a book about her four years with him.

She had a remarkable record as a secret agent and at all times she was directed in her work by this Svengali by whom she was hypnotised. She performed some dangerous tasks, but her most spectacular achievement was to penetrate the extreme right wing organisation of Anna Wolkoff, Captain Ramsay MP and his wife, and the American diplomat Tyler Kent. As a result largely of her work, the Ramsays were interned, and Anna Wolkoff and Tyler Kent were sent to prison. Once, during the trial, she passed close to Anna Wolkoff in the dock. 'I will kill you,' hissed Anna Wolkoff.

She was now sitting in front of me at Claridge's. A matron – there was a feel of faded elegance about her, the wide set apart eyes that I remembered had a touch of sadness; and I had the belief when looking at her that she must have sat on many bar stools. Since her love-hate affair with Max she had had two husbands, but it was Max who still influenced her mind.

So here it was, so many years later, that she was earnestly telling me she wanted to write 'truthfully and honestly about a very strange man who, no doubt about it, had a hypnotic influence over me'.

She never did write the book, for she died a year later. Max, however, did have his story published in a book called *The Man Who Was M* by Anthony Masters. To bring Max to life, however, the story of the love-hate relationship of the very pretty girl who was his secret service agent when in her early twenties needed to be told.

The other incident that I will remember was at the Hatchard's reception, held on the top floor of New Zealand House in the Haymarket, long windows looking out across London – Trafalgar Square, Nelson's Column, St Martin in the Fields, the myriad of rooftops which survived the Blitz, the dome of St Paul's, and the Strand . . .

Jeannie and I stood there by the windows, fascinated by the red rear lights of the cars which went away from us up the Strand, and the dipped headlights which came towards us, when Tommy Joy, the legendary retired managing director of Hatchard's, and Belle his wife, came up to us and said: 'Fred is on the table again.'

He was referring to *A Quiet Year* with its cover of Fred and Merlin looking over a patch of daffodils; and the book was standing with the others on the table of those books belonging to Authors of the Year.

And when Tommy Joy had said 'again', he was referring to the first Hatchard's Authors of the Year Reception, the occasion when *A Donkey in the Meadow* had been chosen as one of the books; and how, on the cover of that book, there had been a coloured photograph of Fred as a foal.

A. P. Herbert was with us that first evening. I remember him raising a glass of champagne and proposing a toast in his delightful bass voice: 'To Fred! Wishing you many, many happy years at Minack!' Another bridge of time.

We were almost home. We had turned the corner by the gate which led to Oliver land, and Jeannie kept on saying, 'Will they be there? Will they have had a fight?'

As every cat slave will understand, Ambrose and Cherry had been constantly on her mind, and my mind, too. In the middle of the night, lying in the comfort of a Claridge's bed, she would have a panic thought that a fox was roaming around the cottage, and both cats were outside, about to be snatched by the fox. There would come a cry from her bed: 'We should never have left them!'

We bumped over Monty's Leap, and Jeannie called out: 'We're home! We're home!' Then on past the stable building on our left, the Orlyt on our right, the headlights beaming their way towards the shadow of the cottage, and to the cherry tree. 'Home!' I called out as I drew up, pulled on the brake, leant over Jeannie to open her door.

It was very dark, very silent.

Then, out of darkness, there sounded a hee-haw, louder and louder, reaching a crescendo that echoed into the night. Fred, in the entrance to the stable below the cherry tree, was giving us a welcome.

'Got the torch?'

'Yes, here it is.'

I gave it to Jeannie and, while I went over to see Fred, Jeannie hurried up the path to the porch. She went inside, opened the door into the cottage with a key, switched on the light . . . Where were Ambrose and Cherry?

Cherry suddenly appeared, coming towards her from the direction of the spare room, showing no surprise. But where was Ambrose?

Ambrose came to me instead. I was nuzzling Fred when there was a sharp yap behind me; and there, as a shadow in the darkness, was Ambrose. I picked him up, and carried him indoors.

It was not until the morning that we discovered Joan's diary of what had happened while we had been away. She had spent several hours a day at Minack, caretaking; and she had kept a record of events. It was headed: 'Happenings at Minack Whilst You Were Away':

Monday

Everything fine – everyone where they should be – no worries. Fred and Merlin in the field by the water trough. Ambrose curled up amongst the bracken, Cherry cosy on the seat in the porch, cosy – until she realised it wasn't who she thought it was coming through the door and then panic set in, but not for long when I kept calling 'Cherry, Cherry, it's all right Cherry – sweeties for you' – panic over she stayed and ate the sweeties, and let me stroke her, purring.

I decided to go and see how Ambrose was getting on – no sign of him in the Orlyt, he had gone for a stroll. So back I went. No sign of Cherry. I suddenly heard a funny noise above me . . . There she was, up on the roof of the cottage by the porch.

Later before I go . . . Birds fed, gulls had their bread, seeds watered . . . Have I forgotten anything? I don't think so . . . warmed some milk for Ambrose, put his fish out for him, although he didn't seem all that interested . . . But he was safely in the Orlyt when I left, Cherry safely in the porch. Must take out hay and carrots for Fred and Merlin. Hated leaving them all alone.

Tuesday

Came down the lane with my usual greeting as soon as I got to the donkeys' gate: 'Fred, Merlin, where are you? Fred, Merlin?' I couldn't see them anywhere . . . They must be all right, otherwise Margaret would have said something (Margaret had collected them first thing in the morning). I'll check properly in a minute, I'll make sure Ambrose and Cherry are all right first. Yes, there's Ambrose in the Orlyt, looks at me, then curls up again. Then I see Cherry running across the path in front of the cherry tree, obviously after something. Nothing alive, just a leaf.

Mind at rest I go back to look for the donkeys. Still no sign, and I have one of my panics again. I went and collected carrots, then followed the path up on the way to the Ambrose Rock. Still could not find them and I began imagining all kinds of things.

Then I suddenly spotted them munching away down in the lower field, so I turned back and went towards them, holding out a carrot. As I got nearer they both came running towards me, Fred a little slower. I suddenly realised I wasn't used to donkeys, and there I was in the field alone with two of them. I decided to give them half a carrot each, then hang on to the other halves whilst making my way back to the gate. So I started back, then found they were trotting after me. I walked faster and they trotted faster. I wasn't really scared, just apprehensive. When I got to the gate I gave them the rest of the carrots, and they were so happy, they let me stroke them, a lovely feeling to touch them.

I got back to find Cherry in the porch. She suddenly seemed petrified, and flew into the sitting room. I had heard the reason for this. Ambrose had come up from the Orlyt and was outside the porch, had seen Cherry, and growled.

Wednesday

No sign of the donkeys. I had been thinking about them a lot because of the weather, it had been a terrible night, and this morning it absolutely fell down and was cold too. On the way down the lane I thought in the distance that someone had a bonfire, but as I got nearer I realised it was because of the sun which was now shining, the heat of it bringing out steam from the land.

What a day it turned out to be, blue sky and very warm, just the type of day as it had been last year when I had finished typing your book and went that beautiful walk to the Ambrose Rock and on along the path when I suddenly heard 'that voice' . . . It was a very quiet day then as now, not a breath of wind, just this lovely, happy old man's voice, no one in sight on sea or land, and I just stood still, I could not believe what was happening, and I retraced my steps to the little bank, and the voice carried on for a second and then was gone. Complete quiet, so still. I know I didn't imagine it.

Got to the cottage and found Cherry curled up in the porch, very contented, stretched out and purring, no interest in the Whiskas I offered, then I found out the reason why. A half-eaten rabbit was under the table. No sign of Ambrose. Then I went back to look for the donkeys, had a hunch they had gone towards the Ambrose Rock, so went up there looking for donkey hoof-marks, taking carrots with me (where would I be without carrots). I found them and they came back with me to the gate.

I found Ambrose later, and he was in his usual place in the Orlyt. I suggested having a talk, but he wasn't interested. I think he is a bit miffed. Cherry seems to like stealing the limelight. What a lovely, dainty little cat she is . . . Noticed some marks, very slight above

145

her right eye. Probably the result of catching that bunny.

The sun has gone. Nasty weather is blowing up. The clouds are gathering fast.

Thursday

A bit overcast but dry and mild. You should have a good journey home. This is the first time that I've arrived and the donkeys are in sight. They came running to me, for carrots of course. How strange they stayed in the field all day, close to the gate most of the time. They know, I'm sure they do, that you are coming home tonight. It's getting colder this afternoon, rain is surely on the way. Everyone is behaving differently. Donkeys by the gate instead of in the field, the gate of the stable field I mean, and Cherry who is usually in the porch, or at the far end lying on the floor by your books, is sitting in your armchair. Never seen her there before. Then when I am about to leave and go outside I find Ambrose coming slowly up the path, and he has always been in the Orlyt before. They are all expecting you. I am sure they are. They are waiting to welcome you home.

'The Diary of an Animal Caretaker,' I said.

'It's so innocent.'

'A lot of people would call it sentimental nonsense. Greed, violence, all the vices are media-exploited, but the love for an animal is branded as sentimentality.'

'What they miss.'

'Love makes people soft,' I said. 'Brittle, ambitious, powerful people don't want to be made soft. They are on guard against love.'

'A bit sharp of you perhaps.'

'I don't think so.'

We went out soon after into the spring air. It was one of those early April days when a gentle breeze brushed the

146

landscape, bringing the sweetness of growing scents. The
sea was quiet. Across the bay, a haze touched the long coastline of the Lizard. A flock of curlews, flying the course their
forebears have taken, flew just to the west of us, calling their
haunting cries. A pheasant cackled in the undergrowth on
the other side of the valley, somewhere in Oliver land,
anticipating by a split-second the boom of the French
Concorde as it flew through the sound barrier on its way to
Paris. A sparrowhawk chased a rook. There was fluttering
in the escallonia where dunnocks were flirting. It was a
morning that held the joy of the beginning of a love affair.
All the blossom time ahead, all the wonder of the first
arrivals: warblers and whitethroats, the first swallow, the
first Red Admiral butterfly, the first cuckoo. A day to
shout to the heavens, asking for nothing, gratitude for
everything. We were home.

We strolled slowly down the path, wondering where
Ambrose might be because we would have liked him
to come with us. We were not concerned about Cherry.
Cherry, as we saw from Joan's diary, reacted to flattery,
played a butterfly, feminine role which bewitched a com-
parative stranger like Joan. Ambrose would never bewitch.
We were his only friends.

It was good that Joan had not witnessed any confrontation between them. There was not a hint in her diary that
they had even stared at each other suspiciously. That was
good. At night, however, both indoors, there may have
been a blazing row, but at least no harm seemed to have
come to either of them.

The donkeys were out grazing in the stable field. Fred,
as we paused by the cherry tree, looked up, watched us for
a moment.

'Later, Fred,' I called out, 'later we'll take you to Oliver
land.'

We began walking up the lane; and the lane was a
dazzling sight.

On either side there were cascades of Coverack Glory
daffodils, their bulbs thrown by us at random many years

before when Coverack Glory lost their market value. How vast was the value which they now gave us, welcoming us home liked a packed crowd, waving yellow, scented flags on either side of the route. There was, too, the exotic scent of the trichocarpa, the poplar which has no flowers but whose sticky buds exude this exotic scent. When we lived at Mortlake in Thames Bank Cottage, opposite the finishing post of the University Boat Race and alongside the Ship Hotel where Gus and Olivette Foster used to reign as land-lords during the war, we used to look across the river to a whole line of poplars. One night, when we were celebrating our first wedding anniversary with a party, a stick of bombs began falling towards us from the direction of the other side of the river. I remember Bob Capa, languid, madly attractive to women, the most famous wartime photo-grapher of all twentieth-century wars, leaning against the front door which was open . . . 'One, two, three,' he murmured, cigarette in the corner of his mouth, counting the bombs in a calm, amused Hungarian accent. 'Now it is us!' And the bomb fell a hundred yards away across the river, blew our roof off, and ended the wedding anniversary party.

There was also a poplar which was a casualty. One of our stick of bombs fell and destroyed it. You can still see what happened. Take a walk to the Mortlake embankment, and look across the river to a spot just short of the Boat Race finishing point. You will see a gap in the burgeoning line of poplars – a memorial to our first wedding anniversary.

We still have a reminder of that night. We have in the kitchen, fixed to the wall above the calor gas stove, a ship's clock, one of those round clocks which are fitted in cabins. Jeannie had asked for such a clock and it was to be my first Christmas present to her; and I had gone down to the London docks and bought it from a ship's chandler. At Mortlake it was in our sitting room at the top of the house; and it was still ticking away after the roof was blown off.

We strolled down the lane, the rush of the past few days

fading away from our minds, and we were coming back to reality, our own form of reality.

We reached the wooden field gate which opens into Oliver land when there was a little strangled cry from behind us, half miaow, half a petulant: 'Why did you leave me behind?'

'Ambrose!' we both cried out.

We turned into the field, and began walking up it towards the gap at the top which led to the Ambrose Rock. The field was called the clover field because, until a very dry summer, it was regularly profuse with clover; and much time used to be spent looking for lucky four-leaf clovers. The clover situation, however, did not concern us this morning. As we strolled, Ambrose pottering behind us, we were watching where we placed our feet, for everywhere was the sparkle of celandines.

We reached the top of the field and turned into blackthorn alley, which on this April morning, was a cloud of white from the blackthorn flowers. Then on to the area where winter gorse still blazed yellow on our left, while on our right beaten down undergrowth led to the elder tree, bare packed mud at its base, the centuries-long home of badgers. We reached the Ambrose Rock, waited for Ambrose to join us; and when he arrived he quickly jumped on to it and, as was his custom, topped it up with purrs.

We returned by the same way, and when we reached the field again, pausing for a moment to look at the cottage, and the wood where many of the trees had become victims of elm disease, Jeannie suddenly exclaimed: 'Isn't that a carrion crow's nest in the middle there, above Boris's house ?'

Boris was the muscovy drake we used to have, and he had his home in a chicken house in the wood.

'You're right, and there's a crow coming in with another stick in its beak.'

Here was an example of our form of reality.

The vulture birds were descending upon the territory of our small birds who filled the summer days with song. Magpies, fledglings hatched, would scour the small birds' nests, so too the jackdaws. It was my annual task to protect the small birds, discover the nests of the vulture birds and destroy the eggs before they were hatched. I did not like the task. I did not like the prospect of it as I stood in the field with Jeannie, Ambrose sniffing at a tuft of grass; and celandines everywhere.

ELEVEN

Each morning I collected Fred and Merlin from the stable field where they had spent the night, and took them to Oliver land. This mid-April morning I found them at the far end of the field, grazing, and when I called them they took no notice; and so I left them there.

Then I stood in front of the cherry tree looking at the pink buds which were soon to burst, no leaves accompanying them, lichen decorating the branches instead, the grey-green curl of the bearded lichen which only grows in the purest air.

I was standing there thinking for no rational reason about friendship; and how delicate it is, first to gain it, then to nourish it. At first, when the promise of friendship seems to be there, you can so easily be shy of pursuing it for fear of being a bore. You know the possibility of this because you have suffered from such a pursuit yourself. Thus the alchemy which creates a friendship requires intuitive responses which respect no rational rule.

I was thinking also, on this particular morning, of the traps which threaten friendship. Never, for instance, take sides in a quarrel; and in particular a quarrel between husband and wife. You can be sure that any word of comfort to one or the other will be used as a weapon; and so, having comforted the one, you will have enraged the other.

I was thinking, too, about the disappearance of friendship, that which was born of propinquity but filtered away when geography interfered, or time. Geography is the less dangerous. Geography, however many thousands of miles apart, will not destroy the memory of friendship. Time, on the other hand, can do so. Time, as people go on their way, divides them from what brought them together.

Suddenly I heard screams from the direction of the cottage.

I ran up the path to the porch door.

'What on earth is happening?'

Jeannie was standing there, wearing tight jeans and a white polo neck sweater, and in the split-second of my question and her reply, I thought how understandable it was that many men have courted her.

'Cherry slapped Ambrose's face – I saw her do it!'

'I can't believe it.'

'I was doing the bending game, placing one saucer by the bookcase for Ambrose, another in the porch for Cherry. After Ambrose had finished, he went into the porch wanting to go out, then as he passed Cherry she sloshed him! And he didn't take any notice, just treated it as an act of a hooligan – quite unnecessary for her to scream!'

The bending game is putting down saucers, picking up saucers. This activity can be performed so often during the course of a day that it should be included in a keep fit book. In the morning as we lie in bed, as Ambrose prowls waiting for breakfast, there will be a discussion as to who should do the bending game. Then, when this has been decided, the one concerned will get up, go into the kitchen, search for the tin opener in the drawer, laboriously turn it round the Best Ever tin, or fork out the coley from its container; and bend. Once, when Jeannie was away, I counted I went up and down thirty times in the day. Quite often it wasn't necessary to bend in the first place. The milk in the saucer was too cold, or too hot, and was left; or boiled chicken was expected to be on the menu, or pig's liver; and so there was a stalking away from the saucer which had required the bending game.

Cherry's behaviour obviously concerned us. Her bad temper, her slapping of Ambrose's face, could be interpreted as a reflex of fear; and it could also be interpreted as a result of the subtle fuss we made of her, the subtle gestures we made to make her feel she was wanted, that she had a home. She may have become overconfident. She may have felt she was the young one about to oust the established one. Human beings can have the same feeling.

In any case, Jeannie and I decided that it must never happen again; and if it did there would be a major black mark in her C Level report, despite the fact I had allowed for an anti-Ambrose attitude in the formulation of her C Level test.

There was now an interruption to the rhythm of our lives. There was the question of dealing with the vulture birds, and among these I include carrion crows, magpies and jack-daws. They are murderers. They will sweep clean a garden of little birds if given the chance; and they will do so in early mornings, soon after dawn, while human beings are asleep. They will fly from nest to nest, picking up the fledglings, then flying them back to their own nests for the benefit of their own fledglings. I have, however, long used tactics that are aimed to defeat their murderous ways without killing the birds themselves. I behave, therefore, in the way of Western society towards murderers. Preserve them.

I followed a policy which favours the pre-emptive attack. Thus I set out to smash the eggs of the vulture birds in their nests; and the success of this policy depends upon me finding the nests, reaching them, then timing my attack on the eggs when the clutch has been completed. Vulture birds have only one brood; and so if I succeed in destroying a clutch, I have succeeded in destroying a vulture bird's family for the whole year.

This April I had a complicated time. It began with a carrion crow's nest so high up in one of the remaining elm trees still alive that I could not plot a way of reaching it. I placed a ladder against the tree, held a long pole in my hand, and failed to reach within several feet of it. Meanwhile, with the aid of my field glasses, I could see the head of one of the crows in the nest; and this meant, of course, she was sitting on the eggs which day by day were coming nearer to hatching. I solved the problem in the end by detaching the aluminium irrigation pipe from one of the greenhouses, all seventy feet of it, then weaving it towards the nest; and weaving it was a true description because it swayed to and fro like a serpent as I held it, one second being near to the nest so that I almost could plunge the end of the pipe into it, the next swaying away sideways. One morning my task was accomplished. The pipe hit the nest, and an egg fell to the ground. Only one. I had mistimed my attack. The carrion crows would be sure to build another nest.

The magpies caused me no problems. Normally I treat their nests as a prime target, and I start scanning for them in the areas of our land before March ends. This year they seemed to have got the message. Not a magpie nest could I find on Minack or Oliver land; and this made me remember an eerie occasion earlier in the year when I saw a concourse of fifteen magpies on the corner hedge of the field above the QE2 field. They spent the day together in conversation, and perhaps they parcelled out each other's areas of control; and our area was omitted as a result of my pre-emptive policy.

A more serious problem developed, however, than the whereabouts of a magpie nest. This April the jackdaws from a neighbouring cliff invaded us. These jackdaws and their ancestors had occupied these particular cliffs for centuries, and now they were being constantly disturbed by climbers. Climbers, brave people, search out lonely cliffs to climb; and they arrive with their ropes and equipment at the base of some cliff or mountain with the admirable intention of proving to themselves that they can overcome a challenge. The jackdaws, in this case, had become weary of the distress the climbers had caused as they scrambled past their nests; and, for the first time since Jeannie and I had come to Minack, they decided their nests should be in the ivy-covered dead elm trees close to the cottage.

The dead elm trees had been chain-sawed about thirty feet from the ground. The object was not to bare a once wooded area too starkly; and so ivy was left to grow up the thirty-foot trunks. An illusion of a tree therefore persisted – an ivy-covered tree.

This illusion suited the jackdaws. Three separate pairs found holes in the ivy-covered trees that made ideal nests. They fooled me for a while. They were so secretive. I would see them hopping among the trees which still had branches, but it was not until I saw one of them disappear into the ivy that it dawned upon me as to what was happening.

I let them remain undisturbed for three weeks, and by that time, I calculated, the full clutch of eggs would have been laid. I was not happy as to what I was about to do, but I consoled myself with the memory of an incident that took place several years ago. A pair of mistle thrushes had a nest in one of the same trees, the eggs had just been hatched, and then a horde of jackdaws descended upon the nest and devoured the fledglings.

My day of action arrived, and I put a ladder against the first ivy-covered trunk of a tree; and up I climbed, hating the task, and fearful, because I am allergic to heights. I stretched out my arm into the hole – and collected five eggs. I put the ladder up against the second ivy-covered trunk of a tree – another five eggs. Then the third – five eggs more, making fifteen in all. Fifteen potential jackdaw fledglings which would have been fed on those of the small birds which nest around Minack. No harm to the jackdaw parents, however, only frustration. I wonder whether next spring they will try again, or whether, like the magpies, they will have learnt a lesson.

Meanwhile we were experiencing drama in the other part of the wood. The two carrion crows whose nest I had smashed had created another; and this time I observed that they had created it within easy distance of my reaching it with a pole. All I had to do was to wait until I judged the eggs had been laid, and then destroy the nest. No pleasure in this either, just a culling necessity to preserve Minack for the robins, the chaffinches, the visiting warblers, dunnocks, the blue tits, the blackbirds and our pair of nesting green woodpeckers. Once I was witness to a horrifying experience concerning a green woodpecker. A pair were bringing up a family in one of the trees close to the cottage, and I had the sweet pleasure of listening to the burble of the young as they were fed. One of the young I particularly noticed because he was always popping his head out of the round hole in the tree trunk. He was the strongest, the bravest of the brood. I was there, by chance, when he made his first flight. It did not last long. I watched a carrion crow swoop upon him.

The new carrion crow nest had, therefore, to be watched, and then dealt with. However, another nest, a huge, bulky nest, had also appeared in the wood some two hundred yards from the carrion crow's nest. It was a nest that gave Jeannie and me huge enjoyment, because, for the first time since we came to Minack, a pair of buzzards had chosen to nest on our land.

The cry of a buzzard, a mew as it is officially described, is one of the most haunting of the countryside. So many times have Jeannie and I been somewhere on Minack land and heard this cry coming from high in the sky, as a buzzard floated effortlessly on an air current. There is a touch of immortality about its sound, as if an angel is singing . . . And now a pair had chosen to build their nest in Minack wood.

'We must stop the donkeys going into the wood,' said Jeannie, 'nothing must disturb them. We must keep well out of sight. You won't be inquisitive, will you?'

The nest was out of easy sight. True, it was low down, which seemed unusual for a buzzard, but it could not be seen unless I crouched behind a grass bank; and then it was yards away, and I had to use field glasses to see any detail.

'I won't be inquisitive,' I said obediently to Jeannie.

Then, as an after-comment, I said: 'What about Cherry? I remember reading how a buzzard dived on a small cat as the cat ambled in a garden, and flew away with it.'

There was silence.

'I'm not imagining things,' I said defensively, 'I'm just thinking that we get rid of the eggs of jackdaws, carrion crows and magpies, and then along comes another predator which is made welcome.'

Still silence.

'Don't you think,' said Jeannie, 'that you are inclined to see trouble before it exists?'

'In this case it is just as well. Just think about these buzzards. They feed their young mainly on young rabbits, and we know that Cherry goes hunting in the wood . . . There is this little cat in the grass, innocently hunting, and one of the buzzards sees it . . .'

'What are you going to do?'

The question stumped me.

'Well,' I said, 'I suppose we'll just have to be hopeful. There'll be probably two young, and they stay in the nest for six or seven weeks before they fly – six or seven weeks when they have to be fed.'

My last sentence sounded ominous.

'You've started me worrying now,' said Jeannie, 'I wish sometimes you were a more complacent person. All the years I've known you, you have always seemed to be on guard.'

'Stupid to say always. It is just that I have never been able to take happiness for granted. Happiness, it seems to me, has to be paid for, some time or other.'

My buzzard concern about Cherry did not, however, materialise; and for a reason that I innocently created myself.

A legendary war exists between carrion crows and buzzards; and a countryman has many times watched the chivvying of a buzzard by a carrion crow. The buzzard twists and turns high in the sky, the carrion crow nearly closing on it; and then it escapes, majestically disappearing into the distance.

On this occasion the war did not take place in the sky, but on the buzzard nest itself. I had waited for the appropriate moment to destroy the eggs in the second carrion crow nest; and this I succeeded in doing – four eggs. I had not, however, guessed where the blame would fall for the destruction of those four eggs.

A few days later there was a commotion of distressed buzzard cries from the direction of the wood. We were sitting on the bridge at the time, having bread and cheese and a bottle of wine. I sensed that a trauma was taking place, but reason stopped me from taking any action. What could I do? So we just sat there, wondering what it was all about.

Previously I would catch sight of one of the buzzards floating down from the sky into the wood from time to time; or Jeannie would tell me she had heard the buzzards mewing. There was silence, however, after the commotion of that lunchtime; and no sign of a buzzard floating down from the sky.

So there came a day when I said to Jeannie that something had driven them away, and though we might be sorry about losing a buzzard's nest, there was the compensation in knowing that Cherry was now safe.

'I still want to find out what drove them away,' Jeannie said. 'They're such huge birds . . . What could have frightened them?'

Thus one morning we went together into the wood, and we stood beneath the empty, bulky nest; and while I was looking upwards to see if any part of the nest had been damaged, Jeannie was scouring the ageless ground underneath for clues.

'I've found the eggs!' she suddenly called out.

Among the natural debris of the twigs and decaying leaves, were the broken shells of large, bluish-white eggs.

Jeannie bent down and picked up the broken pieces, holding them in her hand, and was quite silent for the moment, so silent that a robin singing not far away seemed to bellow into my ears.

'I think I know what happened,' said Jeannie quietly. 'We have always known about the eternal war between carrion crows and buzzards . . . And it is my guess that when you destroyed the eggs of the carrion crows, they concluded their neighbours the buzzards did it.'

'You're being too fanciful.'

'I'm not. It is the only explanation. No animal could reach that nest. There is no human being who knew about it except us. There were only the carrion crows, away at the edge of the wood, who could have a motive.'

'So in a way I was responsible?'

'Yes.'

'One can't win.'

'Oh, yes you did. All around Minack we'll have birdsong this summer. The vulture birds would have won, had it not been for you.'

This experience of nature's jungle war was soon to be replaced by a discussion about civilisation's jungle war.

The cherry tree was now burgeoning into flower, a huge pink cushion; and when one early morning Jeannie and I took a walk to Carn Barges, we stood there looking back across the moorland to the cottage. The sun was rising behind us, and it was shining upon this huge pink cushion which was the cherry tree. Eleven months of waiting; and now for a month the cherry tree would have its time of glory.

On that day I first became aware that we had a wasps' nest in the Orlyt.

A car came down the winding lane in the early afternoon, and pulled up opposite the cherry tree; and out of it stepped a young woman who explained she had come a long way to see Minack, and specially hoped to meet Ambrose.

159

'I was born in London,' she said, 'but now I live in New York. I work in the Secretariat of the United Nations.'

She happened to arrive at a moment when I was in a loquacious mood. Hence, instead of taking her to find Ambrose, I stood with her beside the cherry tree, explaining how I thought the United Nations could solve the world's problems.

'Only the leaders of nations generate talk about the threat of war,' I said, 'and I'm sure they only keep up the momentum of this tension because they love being televised as they arrive at a conference, and when they depart. They revel specially when they are selected for special interviews.

'I suspect, therefore, that all the paraphernalia about arms talks provides the alibi for ego trips. Not a soul wants war among ordinary people. So I have a plan.

'Instead of the superpowers threatening each other with destruction, why not threaten each other with goodies? Think of the possibilities . . . The Soviet Union dropping vodka and caviar on the West, the West dropping kitchen equipment and chocolates on the Soviet Union!

'But, and this would be vital, politicians could still continue to have their conferences. Instead of arms control talks, there would be well-publicised discussions as to whether too many bottles of vodka were being dropped on the West, or too many kitchen gadgets on the East.'

My loquaciousness at an end, I led our visitor to the Orlyt, where Ambrose was lying curled in his customary place in the quay. We stood at the entrance to the greenhouse, and he took no notice.

The young woman from the United Nations, after admiring Ambrose for a minute or two, made a remark which startled me.

'You've got a wasps' nest, just there behind Ambrose . . . But I suppose you knew that.'

I didn't. I had noticed wasps around but I had not associated them with a nest. But now I saw the hole in the hay, a tail's length away from Ambrose's favourite curl-up

160

place where he was accustomed to spend the day, like a long-time member of a London club who expects to sit always in the same armchair.

The young woman from the United Nations departed, having pointed out this new worry; and when she had done so Jeannie and I discussed what we ought to do. Two people had died recently as a result of wasps attacking them. Supposing the wasps descended upon Ambrose?

We decided to do nothing. Leave it to fate. Leave it in the hope that the wasps and Ambrose understood each other; and all that summer they did understand each other. Wasps came in and out of the Orlyt continuously during the day with the speed of bullets; and they ignored Ambrose. Ambrose ignored them, content in the comfort of his place in the hay.

As the days became longer, more and more people came down the winding lane, coming often from distant parts of the world. When I began writing the first of the Minack Chronicles, which was called *A Gull on the Roof*, my sub-conscious purpose was to aim at writing a book which reflected other people's hopes, other people's inhibited thoughts. I had been absorbed in and influenced by the French writer Marcel Proust since I was in my teens. I was jammed with inhibitions, and believed my inhibitions to be unique. Then I read *Swann's Way*, and my life was changed. Other people suffered from the same inhibitions. I was not alone. From then on I have only had interest in writers who can reflect the complexity of human relations; and the complexity of one's own, often contradictory, behaviour.

Those who came down the winding lane, posed us also with a new problem. They might include someone who might claim that Cherry belonged to him or her. I found myself imagining a tearful lady, or a tearful child, arriving at the door, and telling us about this little black cat, whatever her name was at the time, which fled away because, by mistake, the car window had been left open.

'If such a person comes,' I said to Jeannie, 'what is going to be our reaction?'

161

'If they were genuine,' said Jeannie doubtfully, 'I suppose we couldn't refuse to let them have her back. Could we?'

'Of course we couldn't . . . And it would also mean that Ambrose was the undisputed King of Minack again.'

'I realise that.'

'Mind you,' I said, 'I think we should base our longer plans on the results of her C Levels. They are due at the beginning of October.'

'You sound, oh, so solemn.'

A gentle, mocking remark.

'Well,' I said, and I was only trying to be helpful, 'if on the anniversary of the day we found her, October the third, no one has claimed her, I think we are justified in saying she now belongs to Minack. Not to us, but to Minack. She will have become one of the cats of Minack.'

The maddening thing about Cherry was her inclination

to show off to visitors. Ambrose, out of the way, comfortable in the hay in the Orlyt with wasps whistling past him, gave her the chance to take the stage. Ambrose, if he did appear, was always greeted with a barrage of cooing noises. He responded with a look of utter disdain.

Cherry, on the other hand, was flirtatious. A coo noise directed at her might cause her to chase her tail, chase an imaginary butterfly, pounce upon an imaginary mouse, all of which enchanted the coo-maker. I, as an observer, reluctantly tolerated this exhibitionism. If, however, there was any sign that Cherry considered approaching the coo-maker, so that the coo-maker would actually touch her, I would stamp my feet. 'Go off, Cherry,' I would hiss. This attitude was not due solely to my dislike of Cherry trying to usurp the limelight due to Ambrose, but also for a more practical reason. An over-friendly cat can easily be snatched. Cherry, like children, unhappily had to be made to fear present-day strangers.

One C Level test, you may remember, was that Cherry should never bring a live animal, mouse or rabbit, into the cottage. Ambrose in the past had done so, but he had become more careful in his hunting behaviour as the years went by. He would, for instance, capture a rabbit trophy far away up the lane, then I would catch sight of him lumbering his trophy back to the cottage, or rather back to escallonia towers, the base of which he used as a cat restaurant. I would watch him, a huge rabbit dangling in his mouth, crossing Monty's Leap, then tottering up towards me, and on to the restaurant.

The only live rabbit that Cherry brought into the cottage was very small. I was enraged when I saw it, and said it confirmed her departure from us should anyone claim her. A few minutes, however, after my comment, Jeannie captured the baby rabbit by throwing a towel over it; then she carried it outside, up the steps into the Lama meadow, and along to a rabbit hole close to a bench where we sometimes sit. There she dropped it; and it disappeared, like Alice, down into the earth.

I am aware that I can be sometimes very awkward. This was such an occasion.

'How do you know,' I asked Jeannie, and I was still disgruntled by Cherry's failure of one of her C Levels, 'that you dropped the baby rabbit at the right hole?'

There was a look of despair on Jeannie's face.

'Oh darling,' she said, 'what does it matter which hole I left it to go in. I saved Cherry's rabbit.'

We have had many contrasts in values during our lives, Jeannie and I. We both set out in the beginning, when we had left school, to achieve a full life. Both of us had a snobbish element in our characters because we both wanted, unknown to each other, to move into the apparently happy and glamorous world of the famous. Both of us, in our twenties, had this belief that when you were accepted in the fantasy world of gossip comment, and became the cause of such comment, that a kind of everlasting happiness resulted. The true tinsel of such happiness gradually dawned upon us; and that was the reason why we escaped when we were still young; and why, though returning to that sophisticated world from time to time, we can still find far greater spiritual enrichment in the very small pleasures which surround us, like Jeannie's rescue of Cherry's baby rabbit – and whether she put it in the right hole. Or when, that same evening, I fetched the donkeys from Oliver land.

I called for them, and there was no response.

'Fred! Merlin!'

Then, in the far corner where I first saw Oliver about to pounce (he missed his mouse when he did), I saw two white noses in the dusk. A bat flew overhead as I stood there. 'Fred! Merlin!'

Away behind them the Lizard light had begun to flash, and in the bay, although it was still half light, the fishing boats were decorated by port and starboard lights.

Fred began slowly to advance towards me. Why should I be concerned about him? He was looking splendid, a wonderful sheen on his coat, everyone admiring him; and yet there was this nagging instinct within me. Why did he have a speckle of grey hairs on his head. Surely donkeys live forever; and there have been many, many times when Jeannie and I have thought about their future. Supposing we were run over by a bus? What would happen to Fred and Merlin, Ambrose and Cherry? It is a concern which is a common denominator for all who have the wisdom to love their animal companions.

Fred paused for a moment at the spot where he liked to have a mud bath; and as he paused, Merlin trotted past him. Fred, seeing Merlin, changed his mind, speeded past Merlin, and reached me first as I stood at the gate.

As always I let Fred, as senior donkey, go up the lane free of a halter, and then followed with Merlin. An owl hooted, a blackbird, annoyed that we were passing his roosting nightspot, cackled away from us. Fred ahead, me leading Merlin, when I suddenly saw Ambrose close to Monty's Leap. Fred and Ambrose have always been wary of each other, unlike Lama when Penny first came and Fred was a long-legged foal. Lama used to go out into the field where Penny was grazing and rub herself against her leg.

Ambrose now scampered away; and Fred proceeded to carry out his nightly gallop. As he reached the cherry tree he put his head down and, with legs flailing, he galloped to the corner of the cottage, swung right, and stood still by the porch door. This was a routine. This was the moment when he expected, and always received, a special delicacy from Jeannie who would come to the door to give it to him.

Meanwhile I was pulling the halter on Merlin.

'Come on, Merlin,' I urged, adding, 'you will have a delicacy too.'

Such was the difference in our assessment of values between when our careers began, and now.

TWELVE

I had walked to the Ambrose Rock, the donkeys accompanying me, and I was sitting there on the rock, looking back across the dip of the valley to the cottage. It was near the end of May. Around me was the scent of young bracken, and, bordering the path, white stitchwort mingled with the bluebells. I could hear voices from the mackerel boats fishing offshore, and a cuckoo repeating its monotonous call from the direction of Carn Barges. There were other sounds: the harsh, excited trill of a whitethroat, the timeless song of a lark, a blackbird on the branch of a hawthorn proclaiming its love for the world; and there was the hum of bees. To my left along the path, edging it, were buttercups, and numerous varieties of grasses; and there were the seeds of plantain resembling choirboys wearing white ruffs. Opposite me was a glaze of pink campion. Suddenly Fred approached me, then pawed the ground at my feet and pushed his head forward, and began licking my hand.

'Tomorrow is your birthday,' I said.

It did not seem all those years ago when, on 28 May, Fred was born in the field that slopes down to the cliff meadows and the sea; nor does the day when he had a party to celebrate his first birthday, and the children of St Buryan school plied him with ice-cream while Penny patiently gave them rides; nor that day when he took the cap off an elderly gentleman.

'Are those your damned donkeys in the field we've just come through?' barked the man, seeing me standing by the cherry tree.

'Anything wrong?'

'Very much so,' interrupted his formidable-looking lady companion. 'The young one snatched my husband's cap and is running round the field with it.'

Fred stopped licking my hand, and moved off down the path; then he saw a clump of his favourite pink campion, and devoured it.

I stayed on for a little while longer, thinking of the girl who had come down the winding lane that morning. She had visited us two years before on her honeymoon. Today she had come to tell us that her husband had left her. She was in her early twenties, fair and slim. Her husband had gone to work one morning, and never come back. Just a note next day to say that the marriage was over.

We all have moments when we yearn to unburden our pent-up emotions but wonder who to turn to. A friend in whom one confides may tell a friend who will tell a friend. What was a personal secret becomes public property. So Jeannie and I sat with her on the white seat and listened to the girl pouring out her story; and she knew she was safe.

The weather changed during the night, and we woke up to a southerly gale, the window rattling; and by lunchtime the petals of the cherry tree had begun to scatter, like confetti at an old-fashioned wedding. Even the donkeys received some of the petals. They were standing with their backs to the wall in the space in front of the stables; and the petals fell on their backs.

'Spring ended,' said Jeannie.

The rains came and battered the petals which were left; and so by the beginning of June the cherry tree was resembling a faded photograph. Pear-shaped leaves were taking over from the petals – pear-shaped leaves which would still be there when Cherry had her examination results.

'Cherry,' I said, 'has succeeded in her C Levels till now

. . . But there are still four months to go.'

'I'm worried a little about the baby birds,' said Jeannie, 'because there are a lot about. So tempting for her.'

'If I find her catching a single one,' I replied firmly, 'she's out!'

We disappointed the swallows that summer; and I was upset by this because swallows have a special meaning for me. Their flight, from South Africa and back, mirrors in my mind the existence of magic. I hold to magic like a lifebelt. Magic offers hope for the impossible. Reason sets out to prove the impossible is impossible. Reason, for instance, would never have accepted the fact that a pair of swallows will travel from some place in Natal in order to nest in the same nesting spot in Britain as they had done the previous year.

The swallows displeasure was due to an unfortunate incident. As has happened before in rough winters, the felt-covered roof of the outbuilding we call a garage had been badly damaged by winter gales; and there was a rush to repair it in time, hopefully for the benefit of the return of last year's pair. They did, in fact, arrive. They arrived at eight in the morning on 1 May when I was about to take the donkeys for a walk. They skimmed over my head, and into the garage; and then they flew out and on to the electricity cable, chirruping.

I was delighted, but apprehensive. Without our knowledge, and while Jeannie and I had gone out for an hour, the repaired beams had been painted with creosote. The stink was horrible. The creosote had been painted in good faith. The wood beams would be preserved as a result. But what about the swallows?

Our pair of swallows had one brood, and for this we were thankful. The fumes from the creosote could not have been pleasant for the nestlings but, when ready, they flew from the nest. We were puzzled, however, that we did not see them flying around. Generally, after a brood flies, we see them perched on the electricity cable, hear them twittering.

The parent pair did not attempt to have their second

brood in the same place. Instead they changed to the stables, where they first built a nest high up in a corner of the shallow rafters; and when I noticed it I knew it was doomed. Other swallows had built nests up in the rafters, but as soon as the winds blow the roof shifts, and the nest falls. The nest fell as expected on this occasion; and then our pair built yet another nest on a low-level beam, also in the stables. It was within close reach of Merlin's nose. He pushed it over. Our pair of swallows then forsook us.

Merlin, at this time, had fallen in love. It was to be an unsatisfactory affair. The first hint of the situation occurred when we heard a curious noise coming from the direction of Oliver land, like that of an engine grinding without oil. At first we thought it was a steer from Walter Grose's and Jack Cockram's farm which had escaped from its field, come down the lane, and was now calling out that it was lost. I went up the lane to investigate, and on the way looked over the hedge into the clover field whence the sound seemed to be coming. It wasn't a steer. It was Merlin. He stood in quivering alertness, ears forked upright like Churchill's victory sign, his mouth half open, out of which was coming this extraordinary noise. Hootless Mingoose Merlin was trying to hoot.

I was concerned as to what was causing such excitement. Merlin was a highly-strung donkey, in contrast to Fred who was mature, who could face emergencies with calm. Merlin, for instance, was terrified of steers; and on two occasions when a herd of steers had broken into the field where he and Fred were grazing, he had bolted in terror, leaving Fred to face the herd alone, like a stag at bay. Recently I witnessed another example of his terror, although I have no idea what caused it. Something scared him, and to my horror I saw him taking a flying leap at the stone wall just below the lane end of the stables, fail to clear it, and fall sprawling in the lane just as a visiting car was about to arrive. The car pulled to a stop, and I raced down to see what injuries had been done. All was well. He struggled to his feet as I reached him. No injury except a grazed nose.

It was not terror which caused his excitement this time. As the extraordinary noise teetered away into silence, there was a response, in the form of a seductive, lady-like hoot from the top of the hill, in the field which was divided from our land by a waist-high hedge; and I could see, from where I was standing, a little grey donkey. This was the cause of Merlin's excitement. He proceeded to race across the field, as if competing in a donkey derby, sliding to a stop as he reached the hedge; and then he stood there gazing at the little grey donkey rapturously. She was called Nellie.

Nellie had replaced Duncan on the neighbouring farm; Duncan, the friend of Fred and Merlin, who had died the previous summer. She was a very little donkey compared to Merlin. Merlin was a strong, superman of a donkey, capable of pulling a cart, a donkey who would have been in much demand in the days before tractors and cars. Nellie, on the other hand, resembled the beach donkey of picture postcards – also much in demand, but for the gentler task of giving children rides.

She was, I am afraid, a teaser. During the coming weeks of summer, until she was moved to another area of the farm, she was to cause Merlin misery. She would hoot her seductive notes from time to time, informing Merlin that she was up by the hedge and would like to see him. Off he would race to her, stand there gazing at her, only to see her turn away soon after; and he would be left to watch her walk out of sight. Nellie dominated Merlin during those weeks of June and July. He was her slave and she was pleased to have such a fine-looking one. Unfortunately he was a useless slave in her view. Merlin was a gelding.

Fred, meanwhile, observed the progress of this frustrated affair with his usual equanimity. Let the young have fun was his attitude, don't curb them, let them make mistakes so that they can learn from them.

Fred was fond of Merlin, but such fondness could not be compared with his love for Penny. I remember that night when Penny fell ill, and we suddenly heard him, at one in the morning, at the porch door, bellowing hoots, using his hoots like a man battering on the door with his fists. He had jumped the wall by the gate to tell us that Penny was in trouble.

Merlin, as far as he was concerned, was a pleasant companion; and they would go off on forays together which we would watch as we sat on the bridge. Suddenly, although apparently happy grazing in the clover field, Fred would set off to the Clarence meadow, and Merlin would follow. Or he would decide to walk along blackthorn alley, then stop by the badger set that spreads either side of the path leading to the Ambrose Rock. As always Merlin would dutifully follow. Fred was senior donkey. Merlin he treated as a juvenile.

Nevertheless, Fred joined in juvenile games like the matchbox game. I would wrap a box of matches in my handkerchief, then move towards Fred and Merlin, rattling it, and they would co-operate in the game by running away from me as if a demon was after them.

This July, however, saw a change in Fred. Instead of running away when I rattled the matchbox behind him, he stood still. Merlin responded to my game, not Fred. Merlin raced away in delight, flinging up his legs, a demonstration of donkey laughter.

Jeannie, who was with me on one of these failed matchbox occasions, said to me afterwards – an example of Celtic intuition which can be dismissed as sheer fantasy – that Fred was still mourning for Penny. I suppose intelligent animals can be like human beings in that they can forget sadness for a time; and then in unexpected moments it suddenly returns.

How uncanny it is that, as a schoolgirl on holiday, Jeannie used to pass our land when sailing in the *Scillonian* on the way to the islands. There was her future. There was the home she was going to love so passionately.

For me, since the beginning, it has been her courage which has meant our survival. I have never seen her in despair. I can fall into depths of depression, and moan about troubles real or imaginary, but Jeannie, when I have been in one of these moods, has never given a hint of surrender. It is not a bossy kind of courage, it is a very subtle one. It has been sustained by her intense joy in small pleasures. One day in the spring she walked on her own around Oliver land; and when she returned she rushed out these words to me: 'It was so beautiful there this morning, and I only wanted to *feel* the beauty. I just wanted to *feel* the white sprays of the blackthorn, the first bluebells, the celandines and the first buttercups. I just wanted to *feel* the courting of the birds, the clap of pigeon wings, the scent of the gorse, the deep pink of the campion. I was part of all this beauty around me. I *felt* that I was, I didn't think it.'

Then she added.

'How those pundits on TV last night would have despised me for speaking like this!'

The pundits, from the British movie world, had been airing their views as to why the British movie industry had declined, then showing clips from their recently-made movies which explained, not that they realised this, why the industry had declined. There was no feeling in them, no romance – just a superficial gloss.

Of course, Jeannie and I are prejudiced. We are both romantics; and in the use of the word romantic I am embracing the pleasure gained by those slight, honest moments in life that touch the heart, creating a sudden glow which surprises. Such moments may appear to be trivial in the view of the pundits, yet they have their value. They relax those who can enjoy them.

This August, early one morning when holidaymakers were still in bed, we shared together a moment, insignificant though it may seem, that offered a pleasure which million-aires could not buy.

We decided to walk to Carn Barges along the coastal path. This path wends its way through part of our land, though it is well separated from Oliver land. Ambrose, as we set off, was pottering around the flower bed at the base of the cherry tree, and this is where we left him.

Ten minutes later we reached Carn Barges, stayed there five minutes, then started to return for the breakfast of bacon and eggs we had planned. We had gone half way along the path, reached a corner by a decaying elder copse, rounded it . . . And there was Ambrose. He had never been with us on the path before. Instinct had told him where we had gone, a form of love made him follow us; and the result for Jeannie was pleasure beyond the price of a diamond necklace from Cartier's.

The coastal path is an admirable institution because it provides an easy highway for walkers, especially for those walkers who like easy highways and enjoy walking in groups. Sometimes those who walk the coastal path will cause a problem. Campers in particular – they will like the look of one of our bulb fields, put up their tents, and treat the neighbouring undergrowth as a latrine. Among such people there are also those who treat any sign in whatever form it is written, fierce or gentle, explaining the path is public but the land private, as a reason for vandalising it.

One day this August Jeannie and I were together in Oliver land, and looking back across the valley we saw a leisurely walking family of three, father, mother and young daughter.

'What a pretty sight,' I said to Jeannie, 'there's a young family enjoying their afternoon walk.'

At that moment they were passing a notice I had put up on a post a few yards from the path which read: 'No Camping'. Sometimes I have written: 'Please No Camping'. I have also written: 'Very Sorry No Camping'. Each notice disappears within a few days.

On this occasion as we watched the family, we saw the

man walk calmly over to the notice, pull up the stake upon which I had nailed it, and then throw the stake away.

It is an incident like this that increases our anxiety to preserve Oliver land for the sensitive. The sensitive are the losers of this age. The sensitive are aware that moments of solitude can bring a special dimension into one's life, but because they are in the minority, they are always having to surrender more and more quiet places to the crowds.

'I can enjoy society in a room,' wrote William Hazlitt, the nineteenth-century essayist, 'but out of doors nature is company enough for me.

'I cannot see the wit of walking and talking at the same time. When I am in the country, I wish to vegetate like the country. I like solitude, when I give myself up to it, for the sake of solitude.'

Jeannie and I meet solitude-seekers, and we offer them Oliver land, and they go there and find a peace. It is this way of life we want to preserve for decades to come. How can we do so? How can we preserve a corner of Cornwall which is forever free for the solitude-seekers? We ponder about forming a Minack Chronicle Trust; and this I believe we will do. Incidentally, the splendid Minack Theatre at Porthcurno (pronounced Minnack) was known as the Open Air Theatre in our first years; and it is still named as such on the Ordnance Survey Map. I had written three of the Minack Chronicles (pronounced Mynack) when the theatre's name was changed.

September is grasshopper hunting time. Ambrose has always enjoyed it, and the Lama field where we often sit has an abundance of grasshoppers. Thus he will join us as we sit there, occasionally nipping off to Cat Mint Arms which grows in an adjacent, earth-filled hedge, then has a glorious time aiming his paws at a grasshopper, missing, trying again, missing it again; and behaving, in fact, like me when I am trying to catch a fly. On a wall is the offending fly, out comes a rolled up newspaper as a fly swat, down it comes on the fly . . . a split-second after it escapes.

Cherry also liked chasing grasshoppers. She had also

other chasing pleasures. When, as so often, she was sitting on the glass roof of the porch, displaying to us her apricot underclothes, she would tap a paw at a bee buzzing against the inside of the porch glass, or a butterfly fluttering. It was funny to watch the paw tapping while the bee continued to buzz, and the butterfly fluttered.

'Another fourteen days,' said Jeannie one morning.

Fourteen days to 3 October, the anniversary of the day my brother Colin was with us, and Jeannie found Cherry curled at the foot of the cherry tree.

'She's done well, you have to admit it,' said Jeannie. 'Did you really believe when you drew up the C Levels that she would never catch a bird, or bring a live mouse into the cottage? She brought a live rabbit in, I know, but I rescued that.'

'There is still plenty of time for her to catch a bird,' I said, damping her.

Cherry would sometimes hover outside in the expectation of going on a walk with us; and if we were alone she would do so, trotting happily up the lane. Usually, however, she had to stay behind. At the moment we were about to start, Ambrose, possessor of exclusive walking rights, would appear, and Cherry would flee. I therefore decided to make an alternative walking route for Cherry, a route which she could call her own. I took out the Condor, and cut a swathe around the QE2 field. From then on, if they both wanted a walk, Jeannie would go with Ambrose one way, me with Cherry the QE2 field way.

Seven days, five days to go . . . People who had seen Cherry during the summer and knew about the C Level deadline were writing to us, asking for news. We ourselves had been observing these visitors. Was it possible for one of them to have dumped Cherry nearby to the cottage the previous summer, hoping that we would look after her, and now had come to find out if the plan had succeeded? But if she had been dumped, would she have been so thin when Jeannie found her? After a year she was plump and glossy; and the once finger-thick tail was a luxurious black plume.

Four days to go . . . Alan Traynor, the farrier, arrived to attend the hooves of the donkeys. He was tall and dark, a Heathcliff figure brought up in Northern Ireland; and there was a wonderful understanding between him and the donkeys. Sometimes in the past I have had to hold Fred firmly on his halter, and bribe him with chocolate biscuits and carrots to keep quiet. On this last day of September there was no need for bribes. First Fred, then Merlin, stood in the space in front of the cherry tree while Alan Traynor trimmed; and there were no tantrums.

Three days . . . Walter Grose, Pied Piper of cats, came to tell us he was soon to have an operation on his eye. He had lost one eye many years ago, and the good one was fading.

'I was with a man the other day,' he said, 'who was grumbling about the foggy weather we've been having. "Don't you realise," I said to him, "you're lucky to have eyes to see it's foggy?"'

Two days . . . Oliver Hosking, wearing his customary beret, retired member of the longest established flower-growing family in Lamorna Valley, appeared; at that moment I was using my brush cutter to cut the grass in the orchard.

'Wish we'd had that kind of a machine when we had to cut acres of corn with a scythe,' he said; then ruminating, 'Cutting corn with a scythe was governed by the wind direction, always had to keep the wind over the right shoulder. Then by the correct strokes the cut corn was laid out in swathes.'

One day to go . . .

'How are we going to celebrate?' asked Jeannie.

'Celebrate what?' I replied.

'Don't be an old misery. If Cherry has lived through the whole year without breaking any of the rules you drew up for her, you must admit it is a reason to celebrate. Something special for her, I mean.'

'And,' I said, loyal to Ambrose, 'celebration on behalf of Ambrose for putting up with her.'

'Naturally I include Ambrose,' Jeannie said. 'In fact, let's all celebrate. A bottle of champagne for you and me; chicken, which I'm going to roast tonight, for Cherry and Ambrose.'

3 October . . . At mid-day a couple from Capetown came down the winding lane.

'We're going home next week, and we'll soon be seeing swallows flying around our house, for they begin arriving at the beginning of November. They might be Cornish swallows! Could you show us a swallow's nest?'

Although I gave them a welcome, I was aware I may have given the impression I had something else on my mind. I explained what it was, and as I began they looked at me anxiously.

'If a cat called Cherry,' I explained, 'doesn't catch a bird, or bring a live mouse or rabbit into the cottage between now and a quarter to two, a little over one and a half hours time,' I had been looking at my watch, 'she will become forever a Minack cat.'

'Oh, what a relief,' the woman said, laughing, 'I thought it was something serious!'

The couple saw the nest in the garage, then left.

One hour, half an hour, ten minutes . . .

'Where's Cherry?'

'Cherry! Cherry!'

No sign of her.

'I saw her just before the couple went down towards the stables,' I said.

'Cherry! Cherry!'

Ambrose, we knew, was asleep in the Orlyt.

'Cherry!'

Jeannie was holding the two saucers of chopped chicken. I was holding the bottle of champagne and the glasses.

'I will quickly give Ambrose his chicken,' said Jeannie, 'you go on calling for her.'

I walked down to the white seat, rested the champagne bottle and the two glasses against a rock, and went on calling for her.

178

She suddenly appeared, just as Jeannie came round the corner.

It was exactly a quarter to two.

'Cherry,' Jeannie said, 'you've done it! Here is a reward!'

Jeannie walked over to the cherry tree and placed the saucer at its base, the canopy of pear-shaped leaves above her; and in the same spot as when, a year ago, she first saw the frightened, skinny black cat.

I now saw that Fred had joined us for the occasion. Fred was looking over the fence of the stable yard. Fred, who in his lifetime had witnessed the arrival of other Minack cats . . . Lama, Oliver, Ambrose.

I am glad I did not know, at this moment of celebration, what was to happen in three months' time. He had a happy Christmas, nothing wrong with him.

Then, on 2 January, he suddenly died.

The same date, the same place, the same time, as his mother had died, nine years before.

He was buried in Oliver land.

While on the way there, past the cherry tree and up the winding lane, there was an anguished bellow from the field above the cottage. Merlin had found his hoot.